Canterbury, Connecticut Characters
of the Twentieth Century

Cover Picture: George Coombs, taken in December of 1943 in England.

Canterbury, Connecticut Characters of the 20th Century

Sheila Mason Gale
And
Stephen Wibberley

Copyright © 2017 Sheila Mason Gale and Stephen Wibberley

Printed in United States of America

ISBN: 978-0-9832077-7-1

Dedicated to those who have worked
to make Canterbury a better place.

Table of Contents

Foreword

Shortly after George Coombs died, I heard that he had been a highly-decorated soldier from WW II. I was amazed to hear that such a mild-mannered farmer and school bus driver had been such a distinguished hero.

This made me realize that Canterbury residents' histories were dying with them. That thought motivated me to team up with Sheila Mason Gale and write this book. We want to preserve some of the history of Canterbury that is fast disappearing as another generation is rapidly passing on.

The focus is on folks in the 20th century, with some spill over on each end. I am very thankful for the great work Sheila Mason Gale has done in interviewing and writing down the histories of twenty-nine Canterburians.

Sheila and I have chosen the people included quite subjectively, based mostly on those who have been a part of our lives in some way. The order is alphabetical by first name, except for George Coombs, because he is the one who inspired this book, so he gets first place.

The length of each article is determined by how much information we could gather about the person, along with pictures we could obtain, if any.

As this book can be easily expanded, please do give me further information (especially stories) and pictures about those included, and suggest others who could be added. You can email me at stevewibb@pobox.com

Happy reading. May you be inspired and encouraged by these stories.

--Steve Wibberley and Sheila Mason Gale

Introduction

When I (Steve) was growing up in Canterbury in the late 1940s and early 1950s, the town was a true melting pot of nationalities. A look at just Lisbon Road shows this clearly, as many first-generation immigrants lived there.

Going south from Bennet Pond Road, there were the Kinzers from Germany; further along at the top of the hill were the Kuhachiks who were Russians. Pictured below are Mr. and Mrs Kuhachik with one of their three sons, Nick, who was a pilot in the Pacific Theater in WWII.

Down at the next dip in the road on the right was Peter Kuteaka, another Russian. Then at the bottom of the next hill. where Corey Road comes in, were the Pukalos, who were from the Ukraine. Beyond our farm lived Mr. Ginetti who was an immigrant from Italy, and across from his driveway was another Russian family, whose name I've forgotten. At the four corners lived Paula Meinhole Fontaine who had been born in Germany, and came here as a small child. And around the corner on Gooseneck Hill Road was Mike Chyko from Poland.

In other parts of town were a good number of Finnish families, including the Palonnens, Ruuskannins, Saastomoniens and Hakkilas. In fact, I read that at one point nearly 25% of Canterbury were Finnish folk. Along with them were several others of Polish background, such as Ed Waskowitz and Jim Yaworski.

This Old World influx, combined with the long term resident Yankees of English origin, like the Binghams, Baldwins, Tracys and Wibberleys, made for a dynamic and creative town, full of Canterbury characters. And here in the following pages are a good number of them to inspire, entertain and encourage you!

A number of these characters are open about their faith in what they shared with us in our interviews, and we have passed that openness and enthusiasm along.

As you read about George Coombs, count how many times he should have died, but was spared, when so many others in his unit were killed. He was meant to live, return to Canterbury, marry, have children and leave a legacy.

George Coombs 1921-2003
--by Steve

George was born May 15, 1921 in Hanover, CT. His family moved to Canterbury while he was in school. After graduation, from 1939-1941 George worked at the Parks Woolen Mill in Hanover where he operated a machine that produced large spools of thread. In the picture below George is working on his father's tractor.

In November of 1942 he joined the army at the age of 21. When George was shipped out with his infantry unit to go to Africa, after a couple of days at sea, they had to return to port because of problems with the engines. After they were fixed and had set off again, a man was caught putting sand into the oil of the engine, trying to disable it again. George said he was a saboteur, and he was thrown overboard.

After arriving in Africa, George was assigned to the infantry and armored divisions that were going after Rommel. H said the heat in the desert was extreme, hot enough so they could cook an egg on the flat part of a Sherman tank.

At one point, they had Rommel and his forces surrounded in the desert and were waiting for daylight to annihilate them. But during the night a fierce sandstorm came up that reduced visibility to nearly zero. Rommel lined up his tanks single file and had them drive through the American lines under the curtain of sand. The Americans thought the sounds they heard were their own tanks, but in the morning found themselves facing nothing.

George said he did so much shooting in combat that he wore out his carbine; the groves inside the barrel were all but gone, making for inaccurate shooting. He tried to get a new one to no avail. Then, when a high-ranking officer came to visit the camp, George walked by his jeep and saw a brand new carbine laying on the back seat, so he switched it for his worn out one and hurried off with his new weapon. There was also a pair of new combat boots that George would have liked to have had, but he thought he'd better stick to one exchange at a time.

Later in the campaign George's unit came across a pipeline carrying fresh water to the German troops. They decided to switch the water source from the fresh water spring to the Mediterranean Sea's salt water. George was one of the soldiers who put the hoses into the sea. Then when Rommel's forces came to the pipeline to get drinking water and found it salty, they knew they couldn't survive without a new supply of water, and surrendered.

Once Rommel was defeated, the troops were sent to Sicily to fight the Germans there. After landing on the island, they dug in and George was continually reinforcing his fox hole, building a roof of railroad ties over it. And good that he did, because on the third day, a shell landed right on top of it, but he was unhurt, saved by his extra work.

At one point George's group was pinned down by the Germans and ran out of ammunition. They knew that the Germans would attack again and that they would be defenseless. So, George and two others offered to go and try to get more ammunition.

After crawling through the brush to get out of rifle range, they eluded two German patrols and made their way to an ammo dump, rounded up three donkeys and loaded them with ammo. They made it back to their unit just before the next attack came and they were able to hold it off. When asked about this act of heroism and Yankee initiative, George said, "Well, it was better than waiting to die!"

He said there were large snakes in this region and one morning when he woke up, he found that one had crawled in his jacket to enjoy George's body warmth. He leaped up to get rid of it and was immediately shot at; fortunately, the bullet missed him.

As they pushed inland, there were few roads, just narrow paths, so they appropriated all the donkeys in the region to carry their supplies. Since George was a farmer, he was put in charge of a long line of donkeys, all tied together, each loaded with about 200 pounds of supplies. As he led them along a narrow ledge with a steep cliff rising up from one side and a deep drop off on the other, one of the donkeys became panicky and started jumping about. George said the other donkeys all leaned up against the wall, seeming to sense what was going to happen. The frantic donkey pulled loose and plunged over the side. The other donkeys which had braced themselves against the wall were all safe.

By this time, George had been promoted to sergeant and was leader of a machine gun squad. His weapon was a big one which had to be carried in three parts: the breach, the barrel and the tripod.

One day George was walking at the front of the line of his men, carrying the breach, when a shell landed behind him, killing all the others in his unit. The explosion struck him in the back of his leg and knocked him down. The skin of his leg wasn't broken, but he was crippled by the blow.

Shortly afterwards, while he was lying there defenseless, three German soldiers came along and found him. The two younger ones wanted to shoot him, but the older one said in English, "Live and let live." They cut him two sticks to help him walk and put a splint on his leg, got him up and sent him off so he could reach his own lines.

Later he heard that American soldiers had found three German soldiers hung from a tree and wondered if those might have been his three friends who had been punished for helping the enemy.

This injury resulted in George being sent to England for treatment. He went by ship through the Mediterranean Sea, past Portugal to the UK. There he spent some three months getting treatment in the hospital. The picture below was taken during that time in England, in December 1943.

When he had recovered, he was put into training for D day. He said on the original day scheduled for the invasion they were all given a very good meal. But since they were only used to K-rations, the rich food gave them all diarrhea. He said the ship's railing was lined with bare bottoms pointed towards the sea. It was a good thing that a storm came up that night and forced the invasion to be put off for a couple of days so they could recover.

He was in the third wave going into Omaha beach. Because of the heavy machine gun fire, they were dumped off in water over their heads, so a lot of their unit had to drop their weapons and supplies to make it to shore. When they regrouped, out of four machine guns, they only had enough parts for one, and had little ammunition.

Above them a German machine gun nest focused on the next landing craft coming in, and when the door dropped, fired right into it, killing all on board. The driver closed the door and left with his load of dead men. When the following craft came in, George's men gave them covering fire so the soldiers could make it to shore.

One of the problems with the type of machine gun George used was that sometimes a shell would jam in the chamber. One of George's duties was to carry a special

18

wrench to pry out the jammed shell, and for the first time, George had to use that tool there on Omaha beach.

George also heeded his training officer's advice to keep his head down. "Don't be too curious," was the word he remembered. He said that more than one new soldier peeked over the barrier and got shot. "I was willing to wait and see what would happen," he said.

That first night in France, George's unit took shelter in a captured German bunker. They had very little ammo, so feared an attack. But they feared more the possibility of the Germans using a flame thrower to blow fire through one of the port holes in the bunker, which would kill them all. So, every once in a while, their officer would have someone fire a shot to make the German's think they still had ammo. In the morning, they found that among the more than a hundred soldiers, they had only 18 bullets left.

As they pushed off the beach and moved inland, they came to French fields surrounded by hedge rows. They had a special attachment for tanks which allowed them to cut through these thick hedges, and then the infantry could follow. But, George said, you never knew what waited on the other side, so he never wanted to be the first one through the opening; Germans were often hiding in the hedges to shoot you down.

George was wounded in his hand, but after having it bandaged was put right back into action. That night he was sent to guard a road; his partner had been an insurance salesman and George was skeptical about fighting a German patrol with just a "pencil pusher." However, he was spared from action, as no patrols came along that night.

Another time when some English troops were fighting alongside the Americans, George said the Englishman next to him stopped firing so he could make himself a cup of tea on a little stove at the proper time! Then took up his rifle and went on firing.

At one point in battle when all the officers had been killed, George got a temporary promotion to second lieutenant and was told to lead his men on, which he did.

George said that so many soldiers were killed or wounded in his company, that five times the original number of men in his unit came through to replace the dead and wounded; but most of them were killed, too. In the end only a small handful of the original company remained.

They fought their way to the Rhine River where the width and lack of bridges halted their advance. There George was on sentry duty and could see the German sentries on the other side. It was too far to shoot, but they waved to each other. Later a pontoon bridge was built over the river and George road across on a tank.

After fighting continually from June 6 to December 16, George's unit was moved to the Argonne Forest for rest. Ironically, the very next day the Battle of the Bulge was launched right there. The Americans were arranged in a thin line and were totally unprepared for the attack. George and his unit had to run on foot to try to escape from the German tiger tanks.

At one point about 100 soldiers took shelter in a little valley about 8 feet deep where there were small pine trees growing. Just then a group of American Sherman tanks came up on one side of the valley and began firing at the German tanks coming from the other side. George said that the shells were cutting off the tops of those little pine trees.

In the end the German tanks destroyed all the American ones and George's officer told his unit to run. George said that as he ran, he tried to keep away from any groups as the German tanks' machine gunners focused on men gathered together. More than half of the men were mowed down before it was over.

George escaped unharmed for the moment, but was still pursued by the German tanks. On the fourth day of the battle, he was hit by an 88-millimeter tank shell, which badly damaged his arm and side, putting him out of action. He was left for dead, but later someone came by and helped him to a medic.

For all his involvement in combat and his initiative and courage, George was awarded a good conduct Medal, three Purple Hearts, the Silver Star, a Bronze Star, the Bronze

Medal Service Arrowhead, and the Distinguished Unit Badge. He also got ribbons for the American Theater as well as the European and the African-Middle Eastern Campaigns.

When he returned from the war, George was plagued by a reoccurring nightmare where German soldiers where pushing a huge cannon after him, trying to shoot him. When he went to the VA hospital for further treatment for his wounds, the doctor told him that he should talk about his

experiences and that would help to lessen his nightmares. George followed this advice and it did help. It also made it possible to get this information as George told all his stories to his friends and relatives, including Ray Coombs who told me all these stories.

George was asked several times about being in hand-to-hand combat, which

21

he was, but that's where He drew the line; he declined to talk about it.

In the picture on the previous page, George (on the left) poses with his in-laws, Mr & Mrs. Robert Larsen.

In 1947, when the new Dr. Helen Baldwin school was opened, George began driving school bus part time in order to supplement his income from the family farm (pictured below).

In 1961 his grandfather decided to retire from farming, so George became a full time bus driver. Later Dave Ginnetti asked him to be the road foreman for Canterbury and George did that until he retired.

I knew George as a mild-mannered farmer and bus driver. One would never guess that he had been involved in such traumatic and heroic action in the fierce battles of the Second World War and that he had been awarded so many medals for his faithful and courageous service.[1] His example of fortitude, bravery and practicality show what can be cultivated in an ordinary life in Canterbury.

In the picture below, George, on the far right sits with his daughter, Ann Marie (who later served in the Air Force), his mother, Dorothy, his father Harvey (who served in WW I) and his brother Robert (who served in the Korean War).

---

[1] Source George's Honorable Discharge Certificate

As I've thought further about George's story, several of his qualities have stood out, ones that resulted in his surviving so many years of combat.

First, he took advice. When his commander said, "keep your head down," George did so and was protected.

Second, he was industrious and an initiator. Instead of just sitting in his foxhole on the beaches of Sicily, he busily built a cover over his, thereby being protected when the mortar shell fell directly on it. And when his unit was pinned down without ammo, he did something about it. When he needed a new rifle, he did something about it.

Third, he was wisely cautious, for instance, not wanting to be first through the hedges of French fields, as those through first often were shot.

And forth, he was observant, thinking about what was going on around him and what he was doing. For instance, when he was running away from the Tiger tanks, he avoided getting into groups, as that's where the machine gun fire was concentrated.

These are all good qualities for us to cultivate, also. Who knows, in the battle of life, such qualities may save your life, too!

Addison Davis 1916-1996

--by Steve

 Addison, born in 1916, was our mailman in Canterbury for many years, and also worked as a carpenter in town. He built the addition onto the house I grew up in on our farm. The picture on the left is how I remember him in the 1950s.[2]

During WW II, Addison was a radio operator/gunner on a B24 bomber and flew twenty-four missions over Germany before being shot down. He was captured and spent considerable time in a German hospital recovering from his injuries. Then he was put into a prison camp where there wasn't adequate food and many prisoners starved to death.

Ray Coombs related that when the American troops came to the camp, Ray Mercier of Canterbury was among the liberators. He was searching among the bodies for prisoners who might still be alive. He turned over one body and realized it was Addison, in a very weakened condition but alive.

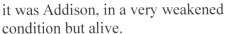 "What are you doing here?" Addison asked.

"I've come to take you home to Canterbury," replied Ray.

Addison, in his military uniform in this picture, was awarded several medals, including the Purple Heart. He died in 1996.

---

[2] This picture and a number of others in this book are taken with verbal permission from the book *Canterbury The First 300 Years* by Amy E. Orlomoski and A. Constance Sear, published by Arcadia Publishing, Portsmouth, NH.

Alex Risavich 1932-
--by Steve

Alex's family moved from Lithuania to the US in 1932 when

Alex was just two months old. This meant that Alex was able to have dual citizenship.

His parents first lived in Brooklyn, New York, where there was a whole settlement of Lithuanian immigrants who had come after WW I. His family then moved to Canterbury in 1934 when Alex was two years old.

Alex's father bought some land on Gayhead Road and built himself a house there. It was quite convenient for Alex

and his brother to walk the short distance to the Gayhead single room school, where he attended from 1938 to 1941.

Alex remembers how his father, who was normally very careful not to waste gas, came in his car one day to pick up Alex and his brother because of a big storm that had started, the hurricane of '38. They made it home without having a tree fall on them, but the powerful winds destroyed their chicken

coop and killed most of their chickens

Alex married his wife, Anita, in 1953 and they had three daughters: Regina, Linda and Donna. He built his own house next to his father's.

Also in 1953, Alex was drafted into the army and was shipped to Yugoslavia as a UN Peace Keeper during the dispute between Yugoslavia and Italy over the city of Trieste. He came home in 1954 and was discharged from the service, happy to return to his wife.

Alex worked for many years as an engineer at the paperboard factory in Sprague, but was an outdoorsman at heart, hunting deer and other game. Here's one of his trophies in the picture above.

I remember him as the woodchuck hunter. He would come and sit up on the hill on the west side of our farm, waiting for a woodchuck to show himself in the big field on the other side of Lisbon Road.

Alex was an excellent shot and could pick off a woodchuck from 280 yards away. He said a good rifle had to be tuned up like a car and his was so finely tuned that from 100 yards, he could put 3 shots into a target within the diameter of a quarter.

When I asked him how many woodchucks he shot, he didn't know the total, but said he got over 100 each year for two years.

I asked him if he'd eaten any, and he related that their meat was light-colored and soft, but not much flavor, while squirrel was tough because it was all muscle. Rabbit meat was soft while raccoon was dark with a strong taste. He preferred deer and antelope.

In his 80s Alex suffered a stroke and is confined to a wheelchair, but he still has a grip that can crush your bones in a handshake.

Aili Galasyn 1930
--by Sheila

In the 1920's Canterbury had a well-established Finnish community when Jack and Ida Hakkila moved here from Brooklyn, New York to be with their friends and have their own farm.

They bought land on Buck Hill Road for $5.00 an acre. Since Jack was an excellent carpenter, he built every building on the property himself, starting with the sauna. He got some help from Arnold Kerr and Ted Dean to dig his pond, as essential accessory to the sauna.

Even before there was electricity and before the roof was finished on the house, Aili (Hakkila) Galasyn was born in 1930. She lives in the same house today.

As a girl, Aili liked to go fishing, swimming, boating and hiking through the woods. She inherited her love for the land and the outdoors from her father. She also had to learn homemaking skills, such as cross-stitch, hand sewing, handkerchief lace and eventually machine stitching. She also became an excellent cook.

When Aili started school, she didn't speak any English, so had a bit of an adjustment. She went two years to the Green School, two years to the North Society Road School, two years back at the Green School and 7th & 8th grade at the Frost school. A few of her schoolmates were: Alice Raymond, June Leiss, Eddie LaFramboise and the Swan boys.

In the spring, the teacher at the North Society Road School would take the children swimming at the old swimming hole on Barstow Road. She also allowed them to go on their own for a hike through the woods and when it was time for them to come back she would ring a cowbell.

In High School, Frannie Gallagher Smith and she became best friends. They often stayed after school to play sports. Since there were no late school busses when they participated in after school activities, they had to take a local bus from Griswold to Plainfield and then dodge a few vicious dogs on the walk back to their homes. Her love of sports continued after she graduated and when she was older, she played in a badminton circuit, traveling around the state.

Aili related that during World War II, a tower was constructed across from the Dr. Helen Baldwin School and was manned by townspeople. Each person who signed up would take a turn to watch for enemy planes. This was done because Canterbury was so close to the shore.

The Finnish people's activities were centered on the Finnish Hall located on Route 169 (N. Canterbury Road), built in 1924-1925. Every Saturday night there would be a dance and her father would play his accordion. All the children had to go because they didn't have baby sitters and this was a nice get-together time for all.

The Finns instilled in their children the value of education. In the early 1940's, women usually didn't go to college, but because Aili was the valedictorian of her high school class, her Mother said to her Dad "let her give college a try". She graduated in 1952 and her tuition each year for four years was $7.00.

She began her teaching career in Stratford and then West Hartford. One of her students, Bob Smith, wrote a book entitled *Hamlet's Dresser* that mentioned her as a young teacher in there.

She started teaching at Dr. Helen Baldwin School in the 1960's when her daughter Katherine was in Kindergarten. One of her classes in Canterbury had 45 students without a teacher's aide. She had to teach reading and English for two periods a day and the reading level was from grade 2 to 12.

She met her husband, Val, when her brother invited him home before they went on a camping trip. They married and had four daughters.

In the early 1940's, Aili's father was on the Board of Assessors. One year Canterbury declared a surplus and the next year the residents didn't have to pay any taxes! This was so unusual the Providence Journal ran a full front-page article about it.

Aili followed in her father's footsteps; when the Republican Town Committee asked her to run as a Justice of the Peace and later as a Registrar of Voters, she won both positions. She was also a Moderator at elections for several years.

She served on the Northeast Regional Planning Agency and that got her interested in Town planning. So, she ran for and won a position on Canterbury Planning and Zoning Commission. Between the two boards, she served twenty-seven years. The Secretary of State honored her with an award for her many years of service.

Aili can remember the many ways Canterbury has changed since she was a child. In 1947, the schools were consolidated into one; the Town government records were kept in someone's house until the 1960's; the post office used to be in a corner of the house near the Prudence Crandall museum. We now have a post office built in 1990 and a beautiful new municipal building built in 2001. Canterbury's roads and bridges have been much improved over the years also.

As for her Finnish heritage, Aili says, "Finnish people were looked up to because they were such hard workers. They knew how to have their fun, and they knew how to cooperate." Aili Galasyn has continued this tradition.

Alice Bingham Baum 1914-2008
--By Sheila

Have you driven down Bingham Road lately? It is a typical country neighborhood, but in 1914 there was only one house on the whole road and that belonged to Byron and Ethel Bingham. That same year, Alice Bingham Baum was born. Over the next few years, Newton, Tom and Dorothy completed the family.

The kids knew how to have fun. Traveling down Bingham Road from south to north there is a bit of an upwards incline and the children would get on their sleds in the winter to slide from the top of the road down and almost reach their house. The boys got some buggy wheels, built a homemade wagon and had a great time riding down the hill.

The Binghams had a large orchard with apples, peach and pear trees. They would can the fruit and put the jars on shelves hanging from the ceiling so, if any mice got in the cellar they couldn't get to the fruit.

Vegetables such as potatoes, squash and turnips were buried in bins in the cellar. They raised chickens, ducks, turkeys, pigs and had cows for milk. Needless to say, they always had plenty to eat. At Christmas it was a real treat to get an orange because, of course, they couldn't grow them.

The Bingham family has lived in Canterbury a long time. Generations of Bingham children attended Gay Head School including Alice when she was old enough.

Her first grade teacher was Nancy Graham, her second grade teacher was Alice Conley and then she had Esther Kimball LaChapelle who was her teacher until Alice graduated.

Alice remembers what a great teacher Mrs. LaChapelle was. She organized a special school program for every holiday and Alice's mother was one of those who made costumes and brought the refreshments. The show would always be in the afternoon and the parents would bring the students' little brothers and sisters to see the show.

There were usually only 16 or 17 children at the Gayhead School when Alice attended. The largest class she remembers was 22 children. On May Day, the first day of May, the children would decorate a big basket (or box) and fill it with cookies and cakes. They would arrive early at school and leave the basket on Mrs. LaChappelle's desk and then go hide in the woods. Mrs. Lachappelle would have to go outside and call them to come into school, but the children would not show themselves until she let them know she meant business.

When Alice went to Plainfield High School in the late 1920's, Warren Hart drove the school bus. He also delivered

the mail in Sterling so he had to have a large vehicle to hold all the mail. In the picture here is his bus; in the back you can see the mail sacks. Students from right to left, Randy, Max and Elisabeth Wibberley with her baratone horn; three unknowns and in the very back in the bus is Sally Havunen. The other high school students called Mr. Hart's bus a "chicken coop" because of its shape.

Plainfield High School drew students from Canterbury, Oneco, Sterling, Moosup, Wauregan and Jewett City. Griswold High School wasn't built until the 1930's.

When Alice was in high school, the minister's wife of the Church on the Green and the Westminster Church formed a girls' club with eight members. Some of the girls who

31

attended were Julia Miller, Marion Safford, Clara Green and Dorothy Hart. They were taught how to embroider and even put on a show for the church on Children's Day. Alice said one of the best parts of the girls' club was making and eating the fancy cookies.

After High School Alice ran a double needle sewing machine at Powell and Alexandria curtain factory in Danielson. When they went on strike, since she had some medical training, she was able to find another job at an infirmary for the aged in New Jersey.

She lived with her aunt in Jersey City and met her aunt's insurance agent, Harry Baum, who would become her husband (seen in picture to left with Alice and daughter Jane). They married and lived in New Jersey for 11 years.

They moved back to Canterbury with their three children Jane, Harry and Walter and eventually built the house where Alice lived for many years on Bingham Road.

Alice became a member of the School Board, as well as the Republican Town Committee and is a long-time member of the Grange. She was a faithful attender of Calvary Chapel.

She was also the President of the Canterbury Senior Citizens and helped to set and accomplish one of the main goals of the group, to have senior housing in Canterbury. Alice also took on the responsibility of organizing the Senior trips. She went on over 150 trips over a sixteen-year period.

When asked how Canterbury has changed since she was a girl, Alice said she loves Canterbury. She knows things have to change because it's just natural that we grow as a community and become more modern. She thinks most people who have lived here their whole life are content with the way

Canterbury has grown.

She said that the people in charge when she was a young person--Charlie Grab, Nelson Carpenter, Milo Appley and Mr. and Mrs. Frink--were always willing to listen to the citizens and worked for the good of the Town. She came back to Canterbury because she wanted her children to experience the same community spirit that she had growing up.

The Bingham siblings: back row Tom and Newton; front row: Dorothy's daughter, Dorothy and Alice

Alice Raymond 1931

--By Sheila

Adelard Raymond and Angelina LaFramboise met while working in the mills in Providence, RI. Adelard always wanted to be a farmer, but he didn't have any experience, but Angelina had grown up on a farm in Canada and was willing to help her husband learn about farming. So, in 1916 they came to Canterbury, bought a farm on Route 169 and started a family.

Angelina gave birth to eleven children, the youngest being Alice LaFramboise Raymond, born in 1931. She was six and half years younger than her brother, Eddie. Her oldest sister Helen and her brother Francis became her Godparents. She feels lucky to still have her Godparents living today.

In First grade, Alice attended the Green school at the center of town, and then throughout her school years attended several different one-room schools: North Society, Frost and Packerville. When she was older, her teacher at the Green school was Georgeanna Wellinghausen who would let the children take turns in walking down to the Frink & Wright store (across the street from Better Value) to get some penny candy.

Her neighborhood pals were the Johnson sisters, Adeline, Mary and Elsie. Also, Aili and Arnold Hakkila. They liked to ride their bikes around the neighborhood including Route 169, Wauregan Road and Buck Hill Road. They would often go swimming in Blackwell Brook and ice skate on the Hakkila's pond in the winter.

Their farm was located near the Canterbury/ Brooklyn line on Route 169 which was the main road between Worcester Massachusetts and New London, Connecticut. Sometimes they would sit out on their front wall and see how many out-of-state license plates they could count.

Her father, Adelard, became very adept at growing potatoes and sold them door-to-door, and to produce markets in Providence, Danielson and Norwich. He also sold them to the government during the war.

Some of their potato fields were just east of the

34

Wauregan Road Bridge. One day, during harvest, Alice's brother drove the loaded truck over the bridge, which was quite rickety. He had just gotten across when the bridge collapsed behind him! The family was then forced to bring all the other potato loads all the way around through Wauregan to get them home. Finally, the town agreed to rebuild the bridge.

Alice didn't have any grandparents, but she had a surrogate grandfather in Andrew Clark, who lived down the road. At Christmas time, he would bring a basket of apples and oranges to the LaFramboise family. That gift was very much appreciated in such a big family and oranges were a wonderful, rare treat.

Alice felt very grown up when she was allowed to walk all the way to Mr. Clark's house with a container of strawberries picked out of the aFramboise' garden.

Arthur Freeman 1927
--by Steve

Art was born in 1927 in Hartford. His brother, Clarence, came

along shortly thereafter to join the family in Canterbury at the four corners of Lisbon and Goose Neck Hill Roads. However, when they were still very small, their mother and father divorced. His mother, Paula, then later married Jerry Fontaine when Art was 7 or 8.

In

the

picture on the right, Art is on the far right, sitting with relatives on the work horse, Frankie.

Art started working early in life, earning 6 cents an hour for farm work. As a teenager, he worked for the town road crew where Newt Bingham was the foreman. When he was old enough, Art worked at the Angus Park Wool Company in Hanover. He also worked for Ted Dean Sr. and Cliff Williams in construction.

When Art was 16 years old and wanted to get a driver's license, his neighbor, Mike Chykow, who knew the inspector at the MVD, took Art down to apply. After Mike told the inspector that Art was his neighbor and a good boy, the inspector asked Art how long he had been driving. Art replied truthfully, "8 or 9 years." So, the inspector gave Art a license without requiring him to have a road test!

Art later returned the favor when Mike needed help. One winter when the weather was very cold, Mike drained the radiator of his truck to make sure it didn't freeze. His bull, unfortunately, found the bucket and drank it all; then he fell over in a heap and lay still. Art helped Mike pull the bull into the barn where they kept it warm, and it eventually recovered.

Art told of another neighbor who, in the pre-chainsaw days, didn't want to cut up his firewood. So, he would put a log in through the window, resting one end in the fireplace. As that end burned off, he would shift the log further into the room until it was all burned up! I'll bet that guy was a bachelor.

Later Art worked for the Wilcox and Harrington Saw Mill. He then applied what he learned there by setting up his own sawmill with 5 or 6 saws and a planner. His best-selling product was oak boards for lobster pots, for which he had lots of customers up from up north.

He was forward thinking and had a chain saw before CL&P did, so they would hire him to cut up trees that came down during storms.

Art married Bea in about 1950 (picture on right). They eventually bought 40 acres up on Cemetery Road, and built a house and barn, where Art lived until 2003. He and his wife had six children—Linda, David, Sheila, Denis, Cynthia and Michael.

Art told of coming home from second shift work late one night and going to take a shower, but found that the bathtub was full of little fish! The next morning, he lined the kids up to find out who had done it. Turned out they all had a plan to stock George Coombs little pond with the fish. Art accepted that with the condition that there would be no more fish in the bathtub. And that evening the bathtub was fish free, but when he went to the kitchen sink, he found that

the fish had moved there. That was it! No more fish in the house!

After building his barn, Art (picture on left) began to raise and sell heifers. A Jewish cattle dealer mentored him in this business,

37

giving him helpful advice and selling him good stock.

Like most small farmers, along with his farm work, Art worked a full-time job to make ends meet. He had a second shift job at Federal Paper Board for over 20 years, which made much of his day free for his other work, including haying. When I was earning my way through college by using my father's equipment to do custom haying, Art hired me to rake and bale hay for him until he got his own baler.

In 2003, he built a new house across the street from his mother's old place on the four corners of Lisbon and

Gooseneck Hill. He lives there now with his daughter, Denise, while his daughters, Linda and Sheila, live on either side of him, his sister, Charlotte, lives across the road, and a grandson lives behind him. A nice family community. In the picture on left, Art in work clothes poses with some of his grandchildren.

As of this writing, Art is 90, still about to get out and walk around, mows the lawn on his riding mower  and enjoys his family. In the picture below, two of Art's old friends, Cliff Williams (left) and John Stringer (middle) celebrate Art's 86th birthday.

Arthur 1926 **and Frances Grab** 1928
--by Steve

Art was born in Plainfield in 1926 and his family moved to Canterbury in 1937.

Arthur's father was a state legislator for 18 years for Canterbury's district. He had a big vegetable farm down on Packerville road where he regularly put in 5,000 tomato plants. For him, Mother's Day was planting day, when he set out all those tomato plants. He also had a large number Brussel sprouts and muskmelons. After he was done picking commercially, he would open the tomato fields for anyone who wanted to pick for canning.

 Frances' father died when she was young and her grandmother took in the three Pellet children. She took them regularly to Westminster church when Phillip Jerome Cleveland was the minister. Francis said Pastor Cleveland was a wonderful man, very kind to her grandmother as she cared for her grandchildren. Francis commented that he preached sermons that stuck with you.

Art met Frances after moving to Canterbury and they married in 1944. Both worked for a while at the Thread Mill in Willimantic.

 Art related how Charles Phillips, who had a sawmill business in town, cut a lot of trees down on Colburn Road and sawed them up there. Art bought a pile of slabs from him, cut them up for firewood and sold it at $5 a cord--his first business venture.

Art joined the Navy in 1944, and was sent to the Pacific Theater. His ship was stationed at Okinawa, but at the end of the war they were sent to Japan and pulled into the harbor of Nagasaki just a few days after the atomic bomb was dropped.

On the return trip to the US, his ship and three others were lost at sea for 7 days in a Typhon. His family heard about it on the radio, but weren't sure if it was Art's ship or not. Then a few days later Frances was relieved to get a call from Art telling her he had landed safely in California.

He got out of the Navy in March of 1946 and came directly back to Canterbury. He and Frances bought their own home on Bennet pond road using the GI bill, and paying $38 a month for the mortgage!

Like many of his contemporaries in Canterbury, Art bought a dump truck, a 1948 Ford F600, and began to haul gravel and sand. He went from town to town, helping as they oiled the roads, working in Scotland, Lisbon, Sterling, Brooklyn, and, of course, Canterbury.

Later he bought a little backhoe and bulldozer to go with his truck. With this equipment, he put in septic systems, foundations and did general backhoe work.

More than one person, among them Arthur LeBeau, described him as a hard worker, accommodating, honest, and doing right by his customers.

Art Grab recounted how, in the late 1940s, Malcolm Wibberley, Merritt Hawes and Milo Appley were the impetus behind starting the volunteer fire department in Canterbury. They used to meet at Bernie Utz's gas station at the Green, where Dunkin Donuts is now. Then they moved their meetings to the grange hall, where they were all members.

Milo went to the bank to see if he could get a loan to build the firehouse; it was approved, and the bank president said any one of the three founding men could sign for it, as they all were trustworthy. However, no one wanted to sign and be liable for it!

So, the fire house was built with all volunteer labor. Art remembers working on it with Fred, George and Elmer Miller, Gus Campbell, Earl Riley and Max Wibberley. Today the old firehouse is part of the Creative Interiors building.

In his earlier years of business, Art supplemented his income by driving a school bus. Denis Yaworski remembers Art being his driver and thought him to be a very old man at the advanced age of 27!

Later Art got tied in with Federal Paperboard and did a

lot of excavating for them. He had a truck–mounted excavator and an impressive fleet of tri-axel trucks. He also had a screening plant in his yard, trucking gravel into his business and screening it there. As one of his projects, he dug the cellar hole for St. Augustine's church here in town.

He told how, at one time, while working in Coventry

he lost the brakes on one of his trucks, and it rolled down the hill and into a house, moving it off its foundation! Art said he was glad he had insurance!

Art ran his business for 50 years with Frances as his unpaid secretary--at that time, by law, a wife couldn't be paid employee of a family owned business.

Now retired, Art and Francis have two children, Mark and Noreen (in picture on left) and seven grandchildren. Francis is very active in knitting and selling her wares at craft shows and other venues.

Art, at 91 and Frances at 89 are healthy, active and mentally sharp.

It must be good to live in Canterbury, as evidenced by the number of residents, like Art and Frances, who have lived so long! Just to name a few, there's Art Freeman and Cliff Williams at 90, Alison Haber at 92, Frances Vaclavik and Art LeBeau at 95, Midge Tyler at 100, Frances Bingham at 101. Her sister, Dorothy Miller, died at 103, Linwood Tracy at 102 and 8 months, Charlie Eastland at 98, Donald Smith at over 100 and Elsie Hawes at 100.

It is also interesting to note that a number of the more successful business men in Canterbury all started enterprises about the same time: Ed Wasko, Eddie Vaclivik, Frank Strmiska, Arthur Grab, Clifford Williams and Max Wibberley.

Art 1922 and Helen 1924-2010 LeBeau
--by Sheila and Steve

If you attended the Dr. Helen Baldwin School in the 1950's, 60's or 70's you probably had a "LeBeau" in your class. Arthur and Helen LeBeau had ten children, and they all attended school in Canterbury. Do you remember Sharon, Joyce, Christine, Arlene, Richard, Gerald, Annette, Marie, Gail or Theresa?

Art was born in 1922 in New Bedford, Massachusetts. His parents later moved to Moosup and he graduated from Plainfield High in 1939

He met his wife, Helen, while visiting a relative in Mass, but made her wait until the end of the war before marrying. They got to know each other better through writing letters while Arthur was in the service.

Art joined the Army Air Corp when he was 18 in 1941. He was sent to radio and radar school and served on B18 planes flying surveillance missions up the coast from Florida, and later out of Trinidad. They were looking for U-boats that were trying to sink ships carrying aluminum ore.

He later went to gunnery school in preparation for B17 raids over Europe, but in the end, was sent to the Philippines where he flew as a radio man on C47 troop carriers. They did air drops of food, ammo and medicine to troops in the jungles. He was then transferred to Okinawa and made flights to Korea.

He was in two Typhoons, one on the ground and one in the air. In the second one, his plane was able to land in the midst of the Typhoon, but the wind blew plane over on the

ground with the crew in it; however, no one was hurt.

He arrived back in the US on New Year's Eve 1945, and went by train across Canada to Fort Devan's, MA. He got out of the army on January 16 and married his wife, Helen, one month later in February 1946.

They moved to Canterbury in 1953 to their present house on Graff Road. They bought the house from Ted and Lydia Greenstein who moved to Tracy Road. The LeBeau house was on the land that had been the Bennett skunk farm many years ago.

In 1953 Mr. and Mrs. Henry Graff were their only neighbors on the road. I (Sheila) used to ride horses along Graff Road and Wright Road with the Graff's granddaughter "Bunny". It is one of the most beautiful wooded areas in

Canterbury. Below is a painting of Art and Helen's house.

Shortly after they moved to Canterbury, Helen got a job at Majestic Metals where they made such things as compacts, rosary beads and lipstick cases. Majestic Metals later became Kaman. Art worked his whole career at Electric Boat as a draftsman and designer.

The family didn't have a TV, but the ten children had lots of activities they enjoyed, like jumping rope, hopscotch and playing in a big handmade sandbox. Their neighbor, Mr. Graff, had a big pond and the children would go swimming in the summer and ice-skating in the winter.

They had chores too, to keep them busy, like weeding the garden. The LeBeaus had three large gardens and grew beans, corn, tomatoes, peppers, squash, okra, pumpkins, peas, carrots, beets, etc. They canned some tomatoes and beets, but mostly froze the vegetables, which lasted all winter. They also had a couple hundred white leghorn hens. Arthur would candle their eggs and sell some of them to his coworkers.

Over the years they also had two pigs and then a steer. Helen was so attached to the steer that, after it was butchered, she couldn't bear to eat any of the meat.

The three oldest girls capitalized on their gardening experience and worked at Verkades Nursery to earn some extra cash.

In 1971 Arthur had someone come in to do some digging in the yard. When the children asked why he was digging, he teased them and said he was building a frog pond, but he was really putting in an above-ground swimming pool!

This pool later saved Art's life. After doing some work with his tractor, Art was refueling it when it caught on fire, with the flames going up his arms and catching his shirt on fire. Streaming smoke and fire, Art raced to the pool and dove in, putting out the flames. He had big blisters on the insides of his arms, but no lasting damage because of the pool.

In the late 50's and early 60's, Canterbury had a school band with Malcolm Wibberley as the bandleader. He generously gave all the interested school children music lessons free of charge. Sharon, Joyce and Christine took lessons and were in the band.

In the picture below is the whole family, taken in about  1964. In the back row: Gerald, Joyce, Christine, Richard, Art, Sharon and Arlene. In the front row: Annette, Gail, Theresa, held by Helen, and Marie.

The LeBeaus attended church in Plainfield, but several people got together in Canterbury and masses were held at the Grange Hall. Mr. LeBeau recalls that Lillian Waskiewicz and Terry Pukalo went to the Bishop in Norwich and asked if a church could be built in Canterbury. They got the approval and St. Augustine was built.

Art told how he and Ed Wasco were asked to be trustees for the church. "Why us?" Ed asked Art, to which Art replied, "Well, I have all the kids and you have the money!" They both had a good laugh about that. Art was a trustee until he was 90.

45

Art could only afford one car and had a big station wagon to hold everyone. Every Friday night they would all pile in and go grocery shopping, then head over to Art's parents to visit. Art would also use his station wagon to pick up other E.B. employees on the way to work and they shared in the expenses, bringing Art a little extra income.

Sharon remembers that, if she had after school activities when she was attending Griswold, she had no one to take her home, so she would start walking towards Canterbury. But she never made it very far before someone she knew would pick her up and take her home.

This changed after getting her license when she was  16. Her mother, Helen, had never gotten a license, but was encouraged by Sharon's example. Art got Mr. Manship to teach Helen to parallel park, and she passed her test in 1964. Then Art got a second car for Helen, and this gave Sharon a way home from school when she needed it.

Arthur decided to run for the Canterbury Board of Education and won. He was on the School Board for six years and was the chairman for two. He had the privilege of presenting Sharon and Joyce with their diploma when they graduated from eighth grade.

Art was also Justice of the Peace for several years, president of the PTA and has served as president of the Canterbury Seniors.

The children were members of the 4-H club, with Richard and Gerald being involved in gardening and the girls in sewing. Sharon learned her lessons well, because today she is still an excellent seamstress. Miriam Pellinen and Elsie Hawes were their leaders.

The LeBeaus now have 18 grandchildren and 2 great-grandchildren. Joyce's son is the father of the two great-grandchildren and she posed for a photo for the Norwich Bulletin showing five generations--Helen's mother, Helen, Joyce, Joyce's son and his child.

When they look back over their years in Town, they

said the biggest changes in Canterbury are the building of the two schools, the municipal building and all the businesses we now have--the restaurants, pharmacy, bank, garden center, etc.

When their children were in their teens and they wanted to go to some activity, they complained to Arthur and Helen about how they lived so far away from everything and always needed a ride everywhere they wanted to go. "Why did you buy a house so way out in the sticks?" they would ask.

Well, when the children got married and had their own families, most of them said, "I wish we could find a place for our family just like this one in Canterbury".

In the picture below, taken in 2004 for Helen's 80th birthday, the whole family is together. Below the picture are their

names, where they live and what they are doing now.

Back row, left to right:
Christine is a retired teacher, living in Georgia
Joyce is a retired RN, living in Georgia
Gerald is a union carpenter and lives in Willimantic
Richard is retired from the Navy and lives in Griswold

Sharon is retired from business in Boston, lives in Canterbury
Arlene is an RN and lives in Meriden.

Front row, left to right:
Marie retired from working at Three Rivers, lives in Plainfield
Annette works for a pharmaceutical company, lives in Georgia
Helen, retired mother
Art, retired father
Gail is a working RN, lives in Westbrook
Theresa works in a daycare, lives in Northfield

Beverly Pukalo
--by Sheila and Steve

Beverly Kettle Pukalo was born in Oneco and moved to
Sterling when she was 11 years old. Her
parents were Ira and Carrie Kettle and
they had eleven children: Walter,
Gladys, Lillian, Norman, John, Eleanor,
Wallace, Donald, George, Beverly and
Harold.

As a child she remembers her
eighth-grade teacher, Julia Miller, who
was from Canterbury.

When the children were all
grown and married, they would get
together at Mom and Dad's on Sundays
and tell stories about their childhood.
Lillian and Donald were the comedians
in the family and would keep the whole
family in stitches.

Every 4th of July the family would gather at Norman's
house in Sterling. He had a grove of trees in the back of his
property where the family would picnic. Some of the family
went quahoging the day before and her sisters would make
two kinds of chowder for the picnic. They played horseshoes
and had watermelon fights at the end of the day.

She met Bill Pukalo, who lived in Canterbury, through
her brother Harold who played baseball with him in the
Twilight Leagues, which would be semi pro leagues today. A
scout asked Bill to try out for the Boston Braves, but he
declined because he was 26 and felt he was too old.

They were married in 1951 and moved to Canterbury
and lived with Bill's parents. It was only supposed to be
temporary, but 56 years later she is still in Canterbury.

When her daughter, LeeAnn, was born, Beverly was
21 and decided she would be a stay-at-home Mom. She
remembers LeeAnn as a child always wanting to be a teacher.
She would sit behind a desk and make her cousin be a student.

And LeeAnn did became a teacher at Dr. Helen Baldwin School.

Beverly was an easy-going person and fit right into this family with the Ukranian traditions and the Russian language of the older folks.

One of Beverly's closest friends was Mrs. Strube, wife of the pastor of Calvary Chapel. Mrs. Strube came to visit her each week and taught Beverly a lot of things she'd never learned in her years of church going, the most important being the need to be born again.

Beverly had always thought in terms of being good to get to heaven, but saw clearly from the Bible that no one could be good enough-- which was why Jesus had to die to be our Savior. Beverly prayed with Mrs. Strube to receive forgiveness, surrender to Christ and was born again; this decision was the most important one in her life and influenced all she did after that.

Mrs. Strube was also the one who got Beverly to start working at the school. Ida Clark and Lucille Bushnell were the cooks for the hot lunch program at Baldwin, and Mrs. Strube worked there for two hours each day to help them. When she had to have her foot operated on, Mrs. Strube asked Beverly to substitute for her.

The school board took note of Beverly's good work and in 1957 Malcolm Wibberley and Helen Laisi took her aside and asked her if she would like to become the school secretary since Doris Becotte Swan was leaving the position.

She passed a typing test and the current Principal, Mr. Ferrell, said she could have the job, but in the end, Beverly said "no."

Later she talked it over with her husband, Bill, and he thought it was a good idea so she decided to take the job after all. However, she told Mr. Ferrell, she would only stay until June.

When June arrived, so did Malcolm Wibberley. One day when she was sitting on the bench in front of her mother-in-law's house, he came by and sat down for a chat. He told her what a good job she'd done and encouraged her to consider coming back in the fall to work full time.

In the end, Beverly agreed and launched into her career of being the "glue and string" of the school. Her work held everything together and her long-term service provided the consistency needed as administrators came and went. She was the Secretary to the Principal/ Superintendent until her retirement in 1994.

Beverly is fondly remembered by the many, many students who passed through Baldwin during her 37 years of work. Her cheerfulness and flexible accommodation of all and her orderliness were key in making the school a pleasant and effective place. She lived out her faith every day in practical ways, like kindness, patience, cheerfulness and grace, in the ebb and flow of the dullness and drama of school life.

When she started at the school there were approximately 325 students. When she retired, there were about 625. In the beginning, the Principal's office contained the desks of the Principal and the secretary, facing each other. It also had a couch for the teachers—this was considered the "teacher's lounge". It was also the office of the school nurse, Ruth Gorman. I remember that just outside of the office, in the hall was a large framed photo of Dr. Helen Baldwin.

It was too difficult for the children to say "Mrs. Pukalo", so one of the teachers, Lillian Goodrich, allowed the children to call her Mrs. Bev. She is still known today by many former students and friends as Aunt Bev.

Bev worked with the following Principals and Superintendents: Edward Ferrell, David Norell, David Boland, Dr. O'Neil, Myrtle Morse, Jim Gallow and Robert Coffell.

She can recall many stories regarding the children, but the following one stands out in her mind.

When Baldwin school was two separate school buildings, some of the children had to have lunch at 11:15 in the morning. Because it was so early, they were allowed to take something from the lunchroom to have as a snack at 2:00pm in the afternoon.

One First Grade teacher found something dripping from one child's lunch box and asked the student what he had saved for a snack. He said he saved his orange popsicle!

Beverly loved the students. It makes her so happy to

have the children, who are now adults, come up to her and give her a hug and talk about their childhood days in school. Sometimes they say they were a "bad" kid, but Bev will always say, "No, you were just a little devilish!"

Bev said God sent Mrs. Strube to introduce her to Christ and to give her a job. She wasn't sure at first whether she wanted the job or not, but it turned out to be one she grew to love for nearly 40 years.

Bill Tyler 1915-1998

--by Steve

Bill was born in 1915 and grew up in Winsted, CT. He had three brothers and four sisters who all became doctors and teachers.

Bill moved to Canterbury at age 22 when his father came out of retirement to became the minister of the Congregational Church on the Green.

Frances Vaclivik said that before Reverend Tyler came, the church was dwindling and he basically saved it. She described him as kind, a people person who loved to visit his flock, where he'd share a Bible verse with each. He was very practical in his advice, a fine person. She also said he was an avid gardener and a hard worker, out there weeding and hoeing on the hottest of days. Eleanor Orlomoski said she picked strawberries for him and remembered him as being a nice man who did a lot with boy Scouts.

Bill wanted to be a farmer, and his father helped him buy a farm on Route 169. He started with one Jersey calf, but chickens were his first big venture. However, the chickens all got sick and died, so he decided to focus instead on milk cows. He bought Guernsey and Holstein cows and built up a sizable herd.

He married Midge in 1938 and they had three sons, Tim, Bill and Daniel. Since Bill was one of eight siblings, he had lots of nephews and nieces who would come to spend summers on the farm and help with the work.

Bill was chairman of the Planning and Zoning Committee for many years. He was known for being very firm in his opinions and his desire was to keep Canterbury a country town, so he sought to encourage "slow development."

Bill was firm, but he was also generous. Alton Orlomoski told of Bill letting him take flat stones off the farm for a stone wall in front of Alton's house.

Two of Bill's sons continue to run the farm, now on North Society Road.

Bob Everts 1941
--by Steve

Today we take implements like weed wackers, leaf blowers and small rototillers for granted, but few know that the developer of all these tools is from Canterbury.

Bob Everts grew up on North Society Road in Canterbury. He was always mechanically inclined, making himself a little three wheeled car out of spare parts in his early teens. One time, when my cousin, Charlie Brown, took me with him to visit Bob, I was allowed to drive Bob's creation on the road.

David Norell's parents were good friends with Bob's, so they have kept contact through the years. Dave gave me the following information about Bob's successful career.

Following graduation from Tech school, Bob studied for three semesters at an aircraft school. Then he moved to

Arizona where, in 1967. he and a partner founded the Rotorway Helicopter Manufacturing Company and began to produce kits for one and two-man helicopters. The picture here is of an early model. To buy land for their operation, Bob sold his 1932 Ford Roadster.

He later sold his portion of the Rotorway company and founded a new one called Piston Power Products. There he put his mechanical genius to work and basically invented the weed wacker, or string trimmer as some call it--including developing the small motor and the head assembly that holds the string. He also developed other small powered implements.

He registered more than 50 patents and eventually built a large factory in Arizona to manufacture his inventions, having, in the end. over 500 employees.

In 1989 he sold the factory and his patents, to Ryobi for 16 million. As part of the agreement, Bob had to stay on as a consultant with the company for five years.

Bob told a story that showed the cultural differences he encountered, working for what was now a Japanese company. Ryobi's new manager came straight from Japan to take over the leadership of the factory with the attitude that whatever was made in Japan was superior. Later when the Japanese manager and his wife had a baby, they brought it to the factory to show everyone. Bob couldn't resist kidding the father, saying that they would have to stamp the new baby, "Made in America!"

Bob continues to live in Arizona where his passion now is collecting cars.

Bucky Burroughs 1942
--by Steve

Roland "Bucky" Burroughs was born in 1942 in Providence, the oldest of three boys, and grew up in Hope, R.I. Sadly, his father was an alcoholic, which made for a difficult life; his father moved his family seven times before Bucky entered high school. To the left is the picture of Bucky's eighth grade graduation.

At the same time, Bucky said he had some good aspects to his childhood because there were ten cousins who lived nearby, so they always had someone to play with.

His father died when Bucky was 15, in his sophomore year of high school. At Thanksgiving that year, Bucky's aunt invited them all over for the day, and when his cousins went to help a farmer down the road, Bucky tagged along. He found he really enjoyed that kind of work, so began going regularly to help his cousins on the farm, first for free, then the farmer, Evert Cornell, hired him for the summer, paying him fifty cents an hour.

At the end of the summer, Mr. Cornell offered him a full-time job, so Bucky quit school and stayed on the farm for the next 4 or 5 years. While working there, Bucky bought some heifer calves and kept them on the farm, and when they began to give milk, Mr. Cornell bought the milk from him.

When Mr. Cornell decided to sell his farm, Bucky rented a farm down the road and moved his cows there. However, now he had to find someone else to buy his milk, which he put into 40 quart jugs.

When he approached another farmer about it, the man said he wouldn't take milk in jugs. Then he asked Bucky's name and it turned out that Bucky's father had been this farmer's milkman truck driver for twenty years. Well that made a difference, so, of course, the farmer changed his mind about taking Bucky's milk.

Later that farmer went out of business and Bucky rented his farm. In the meantime, Bucky's brothers, George and Elliot, joined him in the farm operation. They all also worked for another farmer in the area to supplement their income.

At one point, they were in a financial bind, unable to pay their grain bill, so Bucky, who was 17 at the time, went with his mother to Farm Credit and got a loan. While negotiating the loan, he noticed a nice-looking secretary working there, and tucked that fact away in the back of his mind.

When Bucky paid off all his bills and loans, the grain dealer nominated him for being an outstanding young American and Bucky won that title. He was also in FFA and was Rhode Island's star farmer one year.

The farm they rented was getting too small for their herd, so when a cattle dealer who lived down the road mentioned a farm being for sale in Canterbury, Bucky went over to take a look. The brothers ended up buying Carl Viet's farm on Barstow Road, as Carl was moving to a larger, stone-free farm in upper state New York. So, in 1970 the Burroughs brothers moved to Canterbury, bringing their mother with them.

While hauling the rest of their silage from R.I. to their new farm, Elliot got two flat tires on his truck down on route 14. He didn't know who to call for help so contacted Dave Viet, who told him to call Max Wibberley. Max came right down and fixed the flats. By now Bucky was there and told Max, "We don't have any money!"

"Well," Max relied, "You're moving into town, not out, right? Pay me when you can!"

In buying the farm in Canterbury, Bucky had again gotten a loan from Farm Credit, and had several opportunities to see that pretty secretary, Sue, again. For ten years, he'd been thinking of her and finally got up his courage to ask her to go with him to the Brooklyn Fair, and, much to his relief, she accepted.

When he asked her again for a Sunday night date, she agreed to go only if he would go to church with her. Bucky went, and as he listened to the sermon, he thought for sure Sue had told the pastor he was coming. The sermon touched on all the things that Bucky had been struggling with in his mind—how to handle the difficulties of life, the purpose of life, and how to know if you were going to heaven. He came away from that evening with a lot to chew on.

As Sue realized Bucky was getting serious about their relationship, she told him they needed to sit down and talk about some things. So, they met with the pastor of Sue's church, Pascoag Community.

He was able to give Bucky the answers he was looking for, primarily concerning his relationship with God and how he could go to Heaven.

The pastor explained how each of us is born separated from God, trapped in our natural inclinations to be selfish and do our own thing. We cannot fix ourselves or clean up our sinful tendencies, so God stepped in to provide an answer.

Jesus came to earth, lived a perfect life, then died to take the just punishment for our sins. In His death he bought forgiveness, and in his resurrection, he bought eternal life. These are available for all who choose believe in His being the Savior and choose to surrender to Him as Lord.

Bucky took that step that night, surrendering his life to God, and it turned everything around, bringing the peace and stability and joy he had been looking for. He immediately shared his new life with his brothers and both of them accepted Christ as their Savior and were born again.

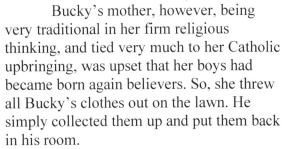

Bucky's mother, however, being very traditional in her firm religious thinking, and tied very much to her Catholic upbringing, was upset that her boys had became born again believers. So, she threw all Bucky's clothes out on the lawn. He simply collected them up and put them back in his room.

When Bucky was planting corn in the field across from Calvary Chapel, where the mall is now, he saw someone walking across the field towards him carrying a mug. It turned out to be the pastor of

58

Calvary Chapel, Mr. Richards. He handed the mug of steaming coffee to Bucky saying, "My wife thinks you need something to warm you up!" In the picture below the Burroughs brothers were harvesting that corn. You can see the spire of Calvary Chapel to the left.

Pastor Richards took to stopping by Bucky's farm after doing his school bus run. This was during morning milking so he could visit with Bucky and his brothers in the milk room.

Then Pastor Richards also began going over to visit Bucky's mother, and quietly, graciously shared the gospel with her. She responded to his kindness and the clear message of salvation he shared, and she, too, accepted Christ as her

Savior. The first ones she told about it were her boys, who were glad. The rest of her relatives, however, were not happy and threatened not to come to Bucky and Sue's wedding, but gave in in the end.

Bucky and Sue married October 20,1973 in Sue's church in Pascoag, RI, and then started attending Calvary Chapel. The first Sunday Pastor Richards invited them for dinner; they were impressed with his hospitality. What surprised Bucky the most about Calvary Chapel was how friendly the people were, with

59

lots of hugs and handshakes to go around.

After three or four Sundays, Margaret Simpson introduced herself and, in her gruff, straightforward way said, "I hope you're going to be more than a pew warmer!" She didn't know it, but that was a very prophetic statement, because Bucky proved to be anything but.

Four or five months after attending Linwood Tracy's Sunday School class, Linwood came up to Bucky and said, "I have to go to Virginia for two weeks for family business. Here, take this book and teach my class for the two Sundays I'll be gone." Bucky was shocked, but took up the challenge, and has been teaching ever since.

Charlie Simpson was the head usher for many years, but when he got sick, he asked Bucky to be the head usher, a service he still provides.

When Pastor Hamburg came in 1975, he asked Bucky to be a deacon, one of the leaders of the church. He accepted this responsibility also, and continues with it to this day.

The Burroughs brothers formed a partnership for their farm on Barstow Road and called it the BZB farm (below).

Bucky learned to be an artificial breeder, both for his own cows and for other farmers' cows. He also learned to take care of his herd's health needs, delivering all the calves, giving intravenous treatments and castrating the bull calves for himself and other farmers.

One time when Bucky was away on an errand, a cow was having a hard time calving, so George and Elliot called the vet, Dr. Sherman. He came but was unable to get the calf out. When Bucky got home, Dr. Sherman said to him, "Here you take a try at this one." Bucky was able to turn the calf's legs and arrange them so he and Dr. Sherman could together pull the calf out backwards.

Dr. Sherman remembered that and one day he called Bucky, saying he was in R.I. and wondered if Bucky could help another farmer in Canterbury whose newly calved cow had cast her withers (meaning her uterus had come out after calving). Bucky used the bottom end of a big coke bottle to push it back in so as not to make any tears in its delicate membrane, then sewed her up using his jack knife and strips of cloth from the farmer's tee shirt. After that Dr. Sherman often called Bucky to deliver calves when he was too busy.

At one point Bucky arranged to keep some heifers on Max Wibberley's farm, but soon got an evening call from Dick Coombs saying that his cattle were up on Water Street. Bucky and Sue, with his brothers, went out and with the neighbor's help rounded up the escapees and took them home. They decided to mow the hay on Max's fields rather than pasture heifers there; it was much safer!

Bucky had always been interested in horses. As a child, he'd watched horse pulls at the fair with his Dad. In the picture to the left in his teens he worked with a neighbor's horse.

In the early 80s he was watching the horse pulls at Rocky Hill State Fair when one of the horse owners he knew asked him to help with the horses. He really enjoyed that and decided to get some horses of his own. He bought a pair from a local farmer, but he said one was a very gentle horse, meaning he wasn't a good puller.

Bucky later went down to Amish country in Pennsylvania and bought more horses, one at a time until he had five. He also bought some horse drawn implements so he could use the horses around the farm.

As the following pictures show, Bucky put his horses to extensive use. Below he's planting his sweet corn patch

Here he's raking hay with a modern but modified side deliver rake.

Spreading manure is a lot more fun when done with horses!

Bucky also used his horses for logging; it was easier getting into small places than with a tractor and wagon.

Bucky also did some side work for weddings at Wright's tree farm. I'd never seen Bucky so dressed up!

However, in the end Bucky said he was glad to do most of his work with tractors. Here his eight-year-old son, Andy, drives one of their tractors.

George and Elliot were not so interested in horse pulling, but got involved with tractor pulls, souping up the tractors to be competitive.

One day after a tractor pull, Bucky was pulling a load of bales from a field back to the farm, not knowing that his brother had upped the pressure of the fuel pump to give it more umph. As he began going up the hill from Ed's Garage to the school, he gave the tractor more gas, and the extra fuel caused black smoke and sparks to come out of the exhaust pipe and set the hay on fire!

Bucky kept on driving because he knew that stopping would mean a big delay. But by the time he turned into Barstow road, he had a police car and a fire truck following him! When he pulled into his farm yard, the fireman put out the fire, but most of the bales were lost.

As the years went by, George began having trouble with pneumonia, and found it was related to an allergy to cows he'd developed, so he left the farm and began working for the town.

Elliot had begun a side business selling farming equipment, which was going well. He decided to leave the farm and opened a store at Westview orchards and eventually

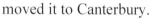

moved it to Canterbury.

In 2000, Bucky was finding it harder and harder to make ends meet. He said he was getting paid 1980 milk prices while having to pay 21st century costs of fuel, parts and utilities that had increased continually over those 20 years.

With these developments, Bucky decided to sell his cows and turned to raising heifers as well as boarding heifers for other farmers. He also raised and sold hay and silage.

Bucky is retired now, although that's not in the normal sense of the word. His son, Andy operates the farm, and Bucky works with him, feeding the cattle each morning, working in planting and harvesting corn, getting in the hay and dealing with customers. Below are Bucky and Sue with their son, Andy, and daughter, Becky.

Knowing what kind of fellow Bucky is, I'm sure he'll be active at church, in farming and in the community as long as he is able.

Charlie Eastland 1911-2009
--by Sheila

In Canterbury's Historical Society calendar, there is a photo

(below) of Safford Mills on Tracy Road near the bridge over Kitt Brook. This mill was established by Joseph Stafford in 1789. In 1920 Edward and Emma Eastland bought this saw and gristmill.

They were familiar with Canterbury since they often came to visit Emma's sister, Lydia Erickson. They liked the town so much they decided to move here and raise a family.

The Eastlands, with their children Emma, Lucy, Ina, Helen and Charles, spent many hours operating the mills which were run by waterpower. The grist mill ground much of the grain for local farmers and the saw mill was just as busy.

Charlie remembers big chestnut logs that were 54" in diameter, but the saw was only 52" high so, after the cut was made, he had to use a wedge on the log to split it the rest of the way.

Besides running the mill, there were lots of other chores to do such as picking apples in the autumn. Charlie says it takes 16 bushels of apples to make 50 gallons of cider.

Charlie walked 1½ miles on gravel roads to attend Frost school. He didn't mind the walk because he always liked to be outdoors. His teachers were Mary Lathrop and Grace Dawley. In the summer, he liked to play baseball, tag, Fox and Geese, and go fishing in Anna Hart's pond. In the winter, all the children would go ice skating on Webbers Pond near the intersection of Bennett Pond Rd and Lisbon Rd.

The section of Tracy Road where Charlie lived was a small "industrial zone". Quite a few of the neighbors had businesses. The Hicks made chestnut shingles and the Smiths made hoops and hockey sticks. When the hoop shop went out of business, they gave all the hoop making implements to Mystic seaport for a display. The Saffords had a pickle farm that sold pickles to the Stanley Company. In 1919 the pickle farm was bought by August Grab who still has descendants in town.

Anyone who knows Charlie knows he's a hard worker. He started work at the age of 14 at the Plainfield Laughton Mills. He became a union carpenter and worked at Pratt & Whitney, Pfizer, the Sub Base, the Coast Guard Academy and even helped build the Goldstar Bridge.

Locally, in 1947 he mixed mortar for the bricks for the Dr. Helen Baldwin School and also worked at a rock crushing plant to build Route 14 between Canterbury and Scotland.

Charlie's grandmother was a vibrant follower of Jesus and often prayed for him and shared her faith with him. He accepted Christ as his Savior under Pastor Gracian, the first pastor of Calvary Chapel, and his wife also became a believer there.

Charlie lived at home until he got married at the age of 28. He met his wife Alma at church and they were

married for 47 years before she died. He said he would happily have had another 47 years with her because she was such a fine woman.

She liked to keep busy and would help with the gardening and even milked the cows at 5:00 in the morning. She once picked 126 quarts of strawberries in one day. Besides their own children, Joyce (Graham) and Mary (Kiddy), they were foster parents to over 25 children.

Mary Eastland Kiddy told of an idea her father had for entertaining his children in the winter. "Drilling a hole in the ice of the cow pond, Dad inserted a large cedar pole and pounded it down until it was secure in the mud; then he bolted another pole to the top so that it would turn. It was about 10 feet on each side of the center pole and we would hold on to the top pole to skate around and around. We would make a

 string of kids hanging onto each other and anyone at the end of the line would get the fastest ride. It is great to recall these things and realize how much he cared." In the picture on the left, Charlie and Alma sit with some of their grandchildren.

Did you know Canterbury once had a skunk farm on Graff Road? When Charlie went looking for a farm of his own, he found a piece of land at the intersection of Graff Road and Barstow Road. He bought the land from the Barkers who told him about a skunk farm that was in operation there in the 1940's. The most highly prized skunk pelts were the ones that were mostly black.

Mary Kiddy, his daughter wrote, "The home we lived on Barstow Road was built in 1710. We had running water but no indoor bathroom. We had two outhouses, one for family and one for company and we had a sauna for our baths. Dad decided he could hook up an outdoor shower powered by gravity feed from a spring fed creek that was 300 feet up a hill in back of the house. He ran the pipe and fed it into a 50 gallon barrel that we could open and close with a faucet...and viola, instant cold shower."

Charlie was an avid gardener. He entered his pumpkins at the Eastern States Exposition over a ten-year period and won first prize eight years in a row. His largest pumpkin was 360 pounds and was ten feet one inch around. He read and studied gardening books to learn the best way to grow vegetables and he once paid $5.00 for one pumpkin seed.

According to an article in the Norwich Bulletin about Charlie's giant veggies, "Getting rid of the monster pumpkins is no problem for Eastlund. He either sells them to a Coca Cola distributor which uses them for displays or he gives them away. He earned about $15 for each pumpkin the distributor bought.

He said he once gave a 120 pound pumpkin to a group of women at a Catholic Church in Waterford to make pies. 'They were really thrilled,' he said, 'I tell you they got a lot of pies out of that thing.' Sometimes he gives the pumpkins to local farmers who cut them up and feed them to their cows. Four years ago, he grew a 109 pound watermelon but it didn't turn out to be very appetizing--the inside was too stringy to eat."

He sold his tomatoes at Michael's Market and Michael Pappas said he grew the best tomatoes of anyone around-- that's because Alma would only send him the very best.

His daughter, Mary, told that when he was selling sweet corn to local stores, he was convinced someone was raiding his cornfield at night. He attached a fishing line to stalks that would have to be walked through to get to the corn, and ran that line through the field and up to his bedroom window with a bell at the end so he would wake up if someone entered the corn field. He never did catch any person and

 realized in the end that the culprits were raccoons.

In his last years, Charlie lived next to the old mill farm on Tracy Road. He enjoyed fishing as well as gardening. Even though he was in his nineties, he couldn't get away from the work ethic he had as a young boy. You could still find him working in his pumpkin patch in the summer sun.

Charles Gallagher Jr. 1932-1964
--by Steve

The Gallagher family, who lived across the street from Westminster Church on Route 14, were friends of my parents, so we often visited.

Their son, Charlie, as we knew him, became a physicist, getting his doctorate from the University of California in 1957.

He said that for the last year of his doctoral studies, he had had to eliminate everything from his life except his work on his thesis: no newspapers, no television, no social interaction, only physics. He was obviously a focused and disciplined individual.

After completing his doctorate, he became a research fellow at the California Institute of Technology until 1959, when he moved to become a researcher in Denmark at the Institute of Theoretical Physics in Copenhagen as a fellow of the National Science Foundation. There he cooperated with some Russian scientists on several papers.

On one of our visits, Charlie told us about the difficulties of learning Danish, saying it was so guttural, that it was more of a throat disease than a language!

Charlie then moved to Columbia University in New York City where he became assistant professor of physics in the Graduate Faculties and was engaged in research projects within his field, charged particles. He also supervised the operation of the Columbia cyclotron in Pupin Laboratories

During this time he traveled to different countries to speak at and attend conferences. Just two months before his death, he'd spent several days in Georgia, U.S.S.R. while attending a conference on nuclear structure.

Charlie, having lived for a long time in Canterbury, loved the out-of-doors and enjoyed bird watching, so he often went for walks in Central Park.

His colleagues warned him of the dangers of New York City, but he didn't take it seriously. One evening he went for a walk, planning to return to his lab later for further work; but he never arrived at the lab and his body was discovered the next morning in Central Park with a bullet hole in his chest.

The murderer was never found, and no clear motive was discovered, as nothing was stolen from his body. There was speculation about some international intrigue, but his specialties and research were not secret or of national significance.

According to an article about his death at age 31, "Charles Gallagher was among the most brilliant and promising of Columbia's young research physicists."[3]

He was survived by his wife, Kristin and two sons age four and six at the time.

Too bad such a productive and highly educated man had to come to such an early end, done in, as it were, by his love of nature.

---

[3] Information and picture from Chicago Tribune, April 16, 1964, and Columbia Daily Spectator, April 16, 1964

Charles R. Underhill, Jr.
--by Sheila

Charles Underhill was a Renaissance man who had many

talents and areas of knowledge. He was a Canterbury resident for 53 years, although he was born in Montclair, NJ and later moved to New Haven, CT.

His father was an electrical engineer who traveled all over the country for his work, so Charles was enrolled in a military

academy so he could stay in one place, and he graduated in 1918 (picture on right).

He then joined the Navy and was the radio operator, or "sparks" as they were called, on the battleship, U.S.S. Pennsylvania, during World War I. In the picture on left Charles Jr shakes hands with his father.

Charles' wife, Frances Barrows Underhill, also grew up in New Haven; she had family who lived in Canterbury for many years before she was born. She and Charles knew each other as children, then they both left New Haven to pursue their careers; but one summer they both returned and got reacquainted, and married in 1923. When their daughter, Alison was born, Charles had a Harley-Davidson motorcycle and took Frances to the hospital in the side car.

Charles graduated from the University of Cincinnati as an electrical engineer and got a job with RCA. He then started to travel the country for work just like his father. The family moved to Bristol, Tennessee and then several towns in Pennsylvania, finally settling in Pittsburg. Charles told his daughter, Alison, he would stay there until she graduated from high school.

Pittsburg was a dirty city then, due to the coal production and steel mills. Alison said any keepsake she has from that time had a dark film on it. After Alison graduated, Charles and Frances moved to Haddonfield, New Jersey (near RCA headquarters) and eventually he retired from RCA in 1953.

At that time, the Barrows farm on Butts Bridge Road, which had been in Frances' family since 1881, was left to Frances and they decided they would retire there. The family was used to coming to Canterbury since they would spend Christmas in New Haven and Labor Day on the Canterbury farm. In fact, they had had their honeymoon partly in this house.

They had the 1787 farm house restored, and today it is being renovated again by Alison's daughter's husband. The contractor who worked for Charles, Mr. Cathcart,

modernized it and added electricity and heat before Charles and Frances moved in. It's present day state is seen in this picture on the left.

They became friends with their neighbors, the Switzers, who were farmers and provided manure for one of Charles' other interests – keeping a very large garden. Frances was good friends with one of their other neighbors, Jean Smith.

Even though Charles had no experience in bee keeping, he researched how to raise bees and, starting with one hive, he eventually had a very large bee business of 10 to 15 hives, selling lots of honey. They called their business, the "Hill Top Honey Farm," with Frances being in charge of the sales department.

Charles would go to the Dr. Helen Baldwin School and teach the children about beekeeping. At times the school children would come to his farm to see the bee hives first hand. At left Charles is in full teaching mode.

He set up an observation hive with a glass wall so his visitors could see the bees at work (in picture below).

He eventually became the president of the Connecticut Beekeepers Association.

After retiring he developed cancer, which the doctors said was incurable. In typical Charles Underhill fashion, he researched t alternative cures and found one using bee products, among other things, was cured and lived many more years.

He also had an interest in history and began to research and

write on the history of Canterbury and surrounding communities. He wrote everything by hand, eventually compiling the history of 46 towns (including one in Massachusetts, one in Rhode Island and the rest in Connecticut).

His daughter, Alison, received a thank you note from every single one of those 46 towns because they were so thrilled to have the information that he had written up.

I (Shiela) as the Assistant to the Canterbury First Selectman, would hand out Mr. Underhill's history of Canterbury to anyone who wanted information on the Town. He also wrote the story for the historical plaque on the green, seen in picture to the left..

His research continued as he became a genealogist and researched his family lineage back to England. One of his ancestors was Captain John Underhill who fought in the 1637 Pequot War between the Pequot tribe and the Pilgrim Colony and the Massachusetts Bay Colony.

Another of Mr. Underhill's interests, building on his Navy training, was being a ham radio operator, which required passing an exam on regulations, electronics and radio operation. He eventually had quite a complex set up, seen in the picture here. Two of his neighbors were also ham operators as well--Mr. Kinsey, and

Malcolm Brown--so he had friends to enjoy this hobby with.

I spent a delightful afternoon talking to Mr. Underhill's daughter, Alison Haber, who is 92 years old. We sat looking out on her yard watching the wild birds and hummingbirds as she told me stories about her father.

Alison moved to Canterbury in 1981 due to her parents failing health. She was a teacher and she told me an interesting story about one of her students.

She had a student in first grade, Suchi, who had to leave the area and relocate to Texas. Alison taught the whole class how to sing "The Yellow Rose of Texas" as a send-off present. Alison and Suchi then had a pen pal relationship that lasted 37 years. They have met in various places over the years and when Suchi had her bridal shower in New York City, Alison gave her all the letters she had written to her.

Suchi attended Alison's 90th birthday party and presented her with a lovely written tribute of their relationship. One of the things she mentioned in the tribute was that Alison has sent her a birthday card every year since 1978 when she was six years old. Suchi now has a doctorate degree in writing.

I wish I had met Mr. Underhill, but I am so glad to be able hear Alison's stories about her father who, after his retirement, took up many hobbies to enjoy and also benefit others. He was a clever, knowledgeable, self-educated man who became an expert in a wide range of fields.

Cliff Williams 1929
--by Steve

Cliff was, right from the beginning, an entrepreneur enamored with machines. As a teen he was always out in the garage working on something. In 1947 when he was 18, he bought a link belt shovel for $18,000 and subsequently used it for 18,000 hours of work. He took it from town to town updating old roads.

In the picture on the left is the same link shovel many years later. Cliff is seated in front and with him are Dennis Yaworski, Bob West, and in the cab Ken Swan, who had run the shovel for Cliff 50 years earlier.

Cliff befriended Dennis Yaworski, even though there was an 18 years age difference between them. Dennis remembers sitting in the cab of that link belt shovel when he was six. He also remembers Cliff as honest, a hard worker and having great integrity.

In 1954 Cliff bought a used Piper Cub plane and later made himself an airstrip out behind his mother's house. Then he bought a used hanger (see picture below) and moved it from Salem to Canterbury. Not having a crane to erect it, he fastened a 25-foot-long tree trunk to the bucket of his link belt shovel and used that to lift the pieces into place.

He flew to Laconia, N.H. one weekend, and while returning encountered a storm. Not having any instruments to

fly by, he set his altitude and speed for a certain number of hours and then came down and was able to land in a hayfield on Ekonk Hill Turkey Farm. Sadly, many years later his son was in a similar situation, but ended up crashing and losing his life. Cliff eventually gave the plane to the Yaworski's Haul of Fame Museum.

Cliff did lots of bulldozer work in the area and had a

succession of big machines, including an earth scrapper, big trucks and a crane.

He was a regular customer of Max Wibberley's tire place, and at one time got into a financial bind so he couldn't pay his tire bill. Max, being an

understanding person, made a deal with Cliff. If he dredged out the swamp on the farm (the upper right corner of the upper picture), they'd call it even. So, in his spare time, Cliff worked for about two years, using his creativity to keep his machines from sinking in the mud. He used old truck tires, railroad ties and iron mats to keep afloat and dug a beautiful pond (seen on the right side of picture on left), which is one of the best investments ever made on the farm.

Cliff did all his own repair work on his machines, often working late in the night. One night the pastor of Calvary Chapel was awakened by what sounded like someone ringing the church bell. He carefully went over to check it out, but in the end figured out that it was Cliff, beating on his Cat D9 axel, trying to get the broken one out to insert a new one.

Snow storms were a good source of income for Cliff.

In one big storm he plowed down Lisbon Road with his dozer, like one in the picture on the left. Note his hanger on the right in the background. In a later snowstorm, he came to Max Wibberley's with his huge payloader and cleared off the parking lot, making snow piles 15 feet high.

Cliff later got a steady job hauling waste for the Paper Board company in Sprague. Dennis sold him a truck that had 2 million miles on it, and Cliff used it for waste hauling for ten more years, and that truck is still in use today.

The picture below was taken on Cliff's 90th birthday--he's sitting in the golf cart on the left, flanked by his sons and grand children--with his original link shovel in the background, the one he bought so many years ago. Dennis Yaworski restored it for him. It is Cliff's positive link to the past.

Chris Alliod

--by Sheila

In 1914, James Richard Aloysius Jones and his wife Christina set up a homestead in Canterbury in the area of Bopp Road and Water Street. They had eleven children. One of his sons, Andrew Jones, married Elina Larson from North Society Road. Andrew was a Railroad Engineer and had to go where the railroad needed him, so Christine (Jones) Alliod was born in New York City. The family eventually moved back to the Canterbury homestead where Christine grew up and still lives today.

Christine's parents did their part to serve the community during World War II. Elina was a spotter and would take her turn at the designated plane watch area across from where the Dr. Helen Baldwin School would later be built. If she saw a plane she would use a phone to report seeing a two or four engine plane. Andrew as an Engineer drove trains that brought troops to their various destinations.

As a child, Christine liked to be outdoors and in the summer she and her friends would go swimming and fishing in Little River. There were a few floating logs and snakes in the river, but that didn't stop them from diving in and having fun. Sometimes she would row out in a boat and fish for pumpkin seeds (small, flat fish) and then her mother, who was a great cook, would make a wonderful Finnish soup with chunks of fish, onions, milk, potatoes and lots of butter.

The Jones' house had been built about the same time as the original Westminster Church and Christine remembers looking at the ceiling and realizing the carpenters didn't use nails, but wooden pegs when they built the house.

The Jones' farm had lots of land, so they were able to raise cows, sheep, chickens and a pig. They also had a very large garden that needed to be taken care of. Chris said taking care of the garden was hard work, but she gained a life-long love of the land from the experience.

Christine and her playmates had fun using their imagination and making up games. She also liked to ride horses and bikes. Christine's closest neighbors, the Coombs family, was about a half mile away. Her playmates were Dick Coombs, Eugene Coombs, Phyllis (Coombs) Cary, Gloria (Coombs) Sharlack, Barbara (Dean) Thoma, Alice Dean and Eleanor Havel.

In the winter she liked to go ice skating and sledding by the Utz and Orr properties. She always liked to hike through the woods and would sometimes come out about a mile and a half away on Bingham Road. Francis Bingham, wife of Newton Bingham, (her cousin) would invite her in for some hot chocolate.

One of the businesses she remembers in her neighborhood was the store at the corner of Water Street and Route 14 owned by Mary and Walter Papuga. Further East down the road from Papuga's store was the location of Canterbury Town Hall/Meeting house. It was across the street from the present municipal building where the Calvary Chapel parsonage is located today. All Town meetings were held at the Canterbury Meeting House until the Dr. Helen Baldwin School was built in 1947.

As a child and teenager, Christine was fearless. She tells of the times she and Cliff Williams would ride his motorcycle in US 95 and Route 1. "The faster the better and

no one wore a helmet in those days."

She met her husband, Martin Alliod, at American Thread in Willimantic. Shortly after they met, he went into the service but they kept contact, and after they were married they set up their home in Canterbury. Marty became very active in Canterbury politics and was the Board of Finance Chairman for many years. I (Sheila) was privileged to be his secretary when he was Canterbury's Probate Judge.

83

Christine is a member of the Eastern Connecticut Land Owners Association and she and Marty planted 3,000 Christmas trees on their property. Every year they must be fed and trimmed and she always enjoys the public coming to tag them for cutting during the Christmas season.

Christine's favorite hobby was always drawing. After her son, Mark, was born she decided to get serious about her art and take lessons at UConn. She also studied with nationally known artists Foster Caddell and Christopher Zhang.

Her favorite medium is oils. She has won numerous awards throughout Connecticut, including the Mystic Outdoor Art Festival, Manchester Lions Club Fine Art Association , and the Willimantic Rotary Art Show. She has become very successful as an artist, and also as a teacher. Her studio is in Canterbury where she conducts private art classes.

In Christine' opinion, the biggest change in Canterbury is the land development. She would advise anyone who owns land to try and keep it in the family because it's the best feeling in the world to walk in the woods on your own property and no one can tell you to get off the land.

Dave Ginnetti

--by Sheila

On March 1, 1980, I (Sheila) started my job as Canterbury's Assistant to the First Selectman. My first of nine Selectman I  worked for, was David Ginnetti. He was appointed as a Selectman in October of 1974 and was elected as First Selectman in November of 1977, serving for three terms until November of 1983. He was very comfortable with public speaking at town meetings and could handle any situation that came up in the office.

His father, Frank, worked for the State of Connecticut as a Highway Construction Manager. His mother, Anna, worked for the Norwich school system as a teacher's aide for special needs children.

One day, while working on the rebuilding and paving of Lisbon Road in Canterbury, Frank saw a man coming out of the woods with a fishing pole. He took a walk into the woods and saw a beautiful pond (here on right) surrounded by pristine land and he liked it so much that in 1934/35 he bought the property from the Meinholds.

 He put up a cabin and a 2-car garage in the late 1930's and eventually put up another cabin and this is the spot where the family would come to in enjoy the summers. But their permanent residence was in Norwich.

One of their neighbors in Canterbury were the Wibberleys. David was the same age as Steve Wibberley and they became good, life-long friends. David can remember many lunches and dinners he and his brother, Dan, had at Max

85

and Virginia Wibberley's big old farm house. There was a house full of kids, so they had lots of summer playmates.

Virginia would often bring the children over to the Ginnetti's pond to swim, and they would spend hours with David and Dan, diving off the raft, playing water games and getting brown in the sun. Virginia and Anna would spend the hours visiting together.

David and Dan also often went over to the Wibberley's farm, where there was always work to be done and everyone pitched in. David remembers working side by side with Steve's grandfather picking up hay bales in the summer sun.

In the winter, Steve would come over with his father's John Deere tractor and plow out the long driveway to the pond for Mr. Ginnetti's renters. It was a good relationship the two families had.

When David was in college in 1967, his parents finally moved from Norwich and settled permanently in Canterbury.

He met his wife when a college friend wanted to buy a used 1955 Chevy and he asked David to go with him to see it. It was a rainy day and as they talked with the car's owner in the driveway, he said, "Go see my daughter in the house and she will get the jumper cables so we can start the car."

The beautiful girl who opened the door was Priscilla. When she started to go get the cables in the barn, David, always the gentleman, said, "No I'll get them for you."

When the friend decided he would go back and buy the car, David, with his positive attitude, said "I'm going with you and I'm going to ask that girl out on a date." Instead of asking her, he told her he'd be by Friday evening to pick her up. She agreed and that set on the path of a good friendship. They have been married now for 47 years.

After getting married, David and Priscilla built their own house on Bates Pond Road, living with their two children in one of the cabins by the pond until it was done.

During his college years David had a part-time summer job working for the State of Connecticut doing road construction. One of his bosses left the state to operate a gas station on Washington Street in Norwich and he asked David to work there part-time as well.

The second year he was there, David met a salesman, Joseph Bruno, who worked for a refining company. He knew David was about to graduate and he offered him a job in the oil business. He said, "Come and ride with me and see how you like it". David thought the job was interesting so he took it and started in the gasoline part of the oil business which included selling fuel oil and lubricants. After a while he started his own lubricants business and then sold it after ten years.

Dave is a very optimistic person and believes if one door closes another door opens. And so it happened, as shortly after selling his business, Dave Waltz, of G. H. Berlin Lubricants, asked him to come and work for him, and David spent the last twenty years of his career with Dave. The company started with one manufacturing facility in Hartford and 10 employees, and when David and Dave retired in 2016, there were 10 facilities and almost 300 employees.

After settling in Canterbury, David would often go the Canterbury Town meetings and express his opinion on any town business that was being discussed. P. B. Smith saw potential in him and approached him to ask him if he would agree to be appointed as a Selectmen, since a current Selectman was stepping down. So at 31 years old, David entered politics.

In 1977 the First Selectman, Lew Gray, decided not to run, so David ran and was elected. The population of Canterbury at that time was about 1,200 with many dairy farms and chicken farms that helped with the tax base. He was a very progressive leader and saw that Canterbury's future included computers for the town government. David proposed the idea to the public in 1983, but it was promptly voted down because the citizens didn't think computers were necessary. Canterbury didn't get computers until 1989.

David and his father were involved in the first study to create Canterbury's Planning and Zoning Commission. He also helped set up the Inland and Wetlands Commission and the Recreation Commission. He is currently serving on the Inland Wetland and Watercourses Commission, and he has previously served several terms on the Planning and Zoning

Commission and the Economic Development Commission.

Another area of activity for David was the Canterbury Associates who developed the land where the town hall, Post Office and mall is. He and Luther Thurlow urged the town to buy this 43 acre lot, but this proposal was turned down. So he and Luther formed Canterbury Associates, bought the land and oversaw the construction done there, including the mini mall with Cumberland Farms. Their efforts have provided Canterbury residents with lots of local services consolidated in one area.

After David retired, he and his wife Priscilla did some traveling. Last year he and the family took a trip to Italy to see the town of his father's birthplace in the Provence of Abruzzo Italy, in the small town of Pettorano Sul Gizio.

David described the Town as a truly Medieval (picture

below). Lots of stone walls, the houses are on top of each other and the streets were so narrow that cars could not drive through them. One of his favorite cities in Italy was Florence. It is a beautiful city with wonderful art and culture. He found it to be a safe city which doesn't even come alive until ten o'clock at night.

David is glad to be living in Canterbury. He reminisced about fifty years ago, when he would come to Canterbury in the summer. It was a more innocent time, but change cannot be stopped, so we must accept what we can, adapt what we can and live out the positive values we've accumulated along the way. That's what will make Canterbury a better place.

David Veit
--by Sheila

August and Maria Grab grew up in Wehr-Oeflingen Germany near the Swiss border. They emigrated to Connecticut and eventually bought a farm in Canterbury in 1919, where they had four children, John, Charlie, Annie and Hilda. Many of the Grab decedents still live in Canterbury today. The youngest, Hilda, married William Veit and they lived with August and Maria in the big farmhouse located just north of the intersection of Tracy Road and Cross Road.

William was a butcher in Plainfield and Hilda was a homemaker, but found time to be a member of the Canterbury Board of Education. Together they had five children: Kenneth, Marilyn (Latham), Glen, Karl and David. Today Karl lives in New York, but the other four children still live in Canterbury.

David Veit remembers growing up on the farm where there was always a lot of work to be done. They had chickens, pigs, beef and dairy cows.

As a boy, he spent time with Henry Tetreault, the Becott children and his cousin, Noreen Grab. They did the usual fun things kids like to do, like swimming in the summer, sledding, ice-skating and ice hockey in the winter.

David was in the first kindergarten class when the Dr. Helen Baldwin School opened. He also remembers that when he was in the fifth grade, Mrs. Alva Lovell was his teacher.

It was a tradition on May Day (May 1st) for the students to put together a basket filled with goodies for the teacher, bring it to school, knock on the door and then hide and watch her find the basket.

Normally after the teacher discovered the May Basket, the children would go inside for a regular day at school. David's class of about twelve students, however, had other ideas. They didn't just hide, they left the school, went down by the Quinebaug River and had a day off. And nobody got in trouble!

David liked sports and played both baseball and basketball. He also played trumpet in a school band. Mr. Dennison taught the music classes in the Dr. Helen Baldwin

School boiler room and Malcolm Wibberley also taught band after school.

As a teenager David got a hydroplane boat from his brother Glen and would race it on the Quinebaug River from Jewett City to above Butts Bridge. He remembers racing against Ron Gluck from Plainfield.

David went to Griswold High School along with his fellow students, who still live in Canterbury: Joanne (Sheriden) Miller, Karvi Ruuskanen, Helen Coombs, Ruth Bassett, Martin Gluck and Julius Vapper.

He then went to Ellis Tech to study tool and dye. The preciseness he learned here would help him later on in his woodworking hobby.

At eighteen he was hired by the owner of Phillips Garage in Plainfield to drive a school bus. His route covered Jewett City, Canterbury and Voluntown.

His community service started early when, at sixteen, he became a member of the Canterbury Volunteer Fire Company. He worked his way through the Company and held  several positions: Secretary, Vice President and President. He agreed to take the Fire Chief position for one year, and every year he would tell his wife, Linda, he was going to take it for just one more year. Well, that one more year became fifteen years— the longest any Chief has held the position.

Speaking of Linda, he met her when his brother in law, Jason Lathrup, said "I bet you can't get a date with Linda." Jason lost the bet and they were married for 52 years.

David was one of the men in the Fire Company who was instrumental in helping Canterbury have its own ambulance. He pointed out that the response time would be quicker and be beneficial for Canterbury citizens if we had our own ambulance. The Fire Company agreed and in 1974

Canterbury got its first ambulance. David became an EMT, and also drove the ambulance as needed.

David became a Selectman from 1983 to 1987. In 1987, First Selectman, Bob Manship, talked him into becoming the Public Works Director. He enjoyed the work and held the job for 20 years.

David continued his public service throughout the years by serving on the Planning and Zoning Commission, Inland Wetlands and Watercourses Commission, CIP Committee, Ambulance Director, Tree Warden, Sexton and President of the Cemetery Association.

In his retirement, Dave is able to spend more time on woodworking projects. He not only creates pieces, but he also restores heirlooms. Mary Bergeron has a high chair that she estimates to be 100 years old, a family heirloom that was used by her father, then her and her children. David repaired it and restored it to its original beauty.

With regard to his many years of community service, David said "the best part of the job was working with the public".

--

Ed 1926-2004 and Lil 1922-2006 Waskiewicz

--by Sheila and Steve

Over a period of time, Canterbury has had several gas stations, or filling stations, as they were called. There was one on Route 169 near the present Cat Hospital, and was run for the owner by Bernie Utz. Later Bernie went into business for himself moving to where Dunkin Donuts is today.

The Papuga family had a station near the intersection of Route 14 and Water Street. Another station was named The Red Dome, and was originally owned by Mr. Gaskill on Route 169 near the Kinsey house. Becottes, located where Bergeron Limited is today, is another station I (Sheila) remember very well because our school bus would stop there on our way back from Griswold High School. However, the longest lasting gas station/garage in Canterbury is Ed's Garage, which has been in business since 1946.

Edward Waskiewicz was born in Canterbury in 1926 and grew up on his family's farm on Lisbon Road. His parents  Walter and Martha had been farmers in Poland and came to America via Ellis Island. They eventually bought the farm on Lisbon Road where Ed and his brothers and sister were raised. Ed said the farm had a little bit of everything--a garden, cows, chickens, and other farm animals, including the pony he's riding in this picture..

Ed attended the Frost School, the School on the Green and then Griswold High School. He liked to dance and went to all the Polish dances in the area. He met his wife, Lillian, at a dance in Moosup where she was collecting tickets at the door. Lillian said she liked Ed right away, while Ed said Lillian and her sisters were all nice looking girls and he wasn't sure which one to pick, but in the end he chose Lillian. This turned out to be a smart move, as she was a great help to him in all his ventures in business..

He had learned to be a mechanic on the farm and when he went into the service, he worked as a mechanic in the Korean conflict.

When he got back from the Korean War, he bought his first dump truck and started his trucking business. He bought the property where Ed's Garage now stands from Walter Peck, who was a schoolteacher in New London. Lillian kept the books, and did whatever else that was needed for the business, including pumping gas when Ed was away.

He was eventually able to hire help, the first being Cliff Coombs who was his mechanic for several years; later Howard Hart joined him. Following that, many young people worked for Ed and Lillian at the garage--Charles Anthony, Ron Robinson, David and Jeff Strmiska and Larry Laisi, just to name a few.

Marguerite Tracy Simpson worked in the office with Lillian and it was Marguerite who encouraged Ed to run for political office. He ran and was elected First Selectman three times between 1963 and 1969. He did the job for free because he felt he wanted to give something back to the Town.

One of the things he is proud of are the roads he constructed when in office. The more roads a town has, the more state grant money it receives. This is still true today. Ed, with the help of Cliff Williams, Arthur Grab and town workers, cleared and constructed Buntz, Cory, Kitt, and Howe Roads.

He also served the Town as an assistant Fire Chief and was a Charter Member of the Volunteer Fire Company.

Ed became interested in horses when he bought one for his daughter and a pony for his son, so he decided to raise quarter horses. Here's Ed riding one of his steeds.

He went to a horse auction in Texas to bid on the King Horse Line of quarter horses.

He bought 16 horses, which made the Texans unhappy because they didn't think these quarter horses should leave Texas for Connecticut. He bred, showed and entered his horses in various events. My (Shelia) childhood friend, Linda Bassett, rode Ed's horses in barrel racing competitions. One of his horses, Mr. Wimpy Leo, became a world champion.

He was also a car racing enthusiast and his car won the

 championship trophy in the Non-Ford Division at Waterford speedway. His drivers were George LaChapelle (in picture on left) and Lew Tetreault. Not only did he like fast cars, but he collected antique cars and trucks as well.

Edward and Lillian Waskiewicz started a booming business with one dump truck and added the gas station, heating oil, horses and a gravel bank. Ed had vision and always strived to improve his business and his life

His heating oil business remained the mainstay of his enterprises. He was a dependable source of heating oil because he kept a big supply on hand in the tanks behind his gas station. And his fleet of service vans kept all his customers warm and cozy. His moto, "Ed's fleet delivers the heat," was true.

Ed and Lil were very community minded and generous in their giving. When the Congregational Church on the green burned to the ground, Ed and Lil gave freely to help get it rebuilt, although they themselves were strong Catholics.

They were part of the movement to have St. Augustine's Church built in Canterbury. Ed and Art LeBeau were the first trustees for the church.

Ed was a pretty humble, down to earth guy. Dave Norell said Ed was always in work clothes, "ready to clean a furnace at the drop of a hat." Charlie Anthony told Dave how he went with Ed to the Foxburough Peterbilt dealer. The salesman there took one look at Ed in his work clothes and brushed him off. Ed just calmly asked for the manager and was ushered into his office.

An hour later he and Charlie came out and as they were leaving, heard the salesman ask the manager, "Who is that hobo?" The manager replied "That hobo was Mr. Waskiewicz and he just bought three trucks. Too bad you missed getting the commission!"

Al Olomorski told how in his later years Ed developed diabetes and had to have one leg amputated. Al made it a point to visit him weekly and take him out. He said Ed never complained at all about his missing leg and could laugh at the problems he had with his artificial leg, like the time he got it on backwards, or when it fell off under the table while they were having lunch. Shows the good sense of humor and positive attitude Ed had cultivated through his life.

Ed and Lil, shown below at their 50th wedding anniversary, certainly affected in many positive ways many lives both individually and as a community over their life times. They made Canterbury a better place to live.

Some further pictures of Ed and Lil

Above left, Ed and Lil receiving the trophy for winning the championship at Waterford Speed Bowl. Middle, Ed and Lil in their early years together. Right, Ed and an army buddy in Korea.

Ed's furnace repair trucks are a common sight in Canterbury and always has enough fuel because he keeps a large stock of heating oil in the big neat row of tanks behind the garage.

Ed Vaclavick 1922-2006
--by Steve

Ed was another one of those entrepreneurs, an easy going, creative man who had several careers. Born in 1922 in southern Connecticut, he quit high school after his sophomore year in order to help support his mother. His first job was driving a coal truck to and from Pennsylvania. He didn't have a driver's license, but that was no problem for him, he had a job to do and did it.

After serving in the Pacific Theatre during World War II as an airplane mechanic (prop specialist), he had trouble adjusting to the cold weather of New England, so he went to

live with his sister in Florida.

While at a gas station, he gallantly opened the door for two girls, one of whom was from Canterbury. Frances Lovell had gone down to visit friends and enjoy the warm weather.

Eddie was taken by this tall, slim and elegant girl (see picture on the left) and followed her back to Connecticut where they were married one year later in 1948. He didn't bother to ask her, just announced that they were going to get married!

They settled down in Canterbury on the farm that Frances's grandfather had bought years before and eventually in 1961 built a house for themselves there on Route 14 just down below the Green. Ed, of course, dug a pond to make it more beautiful (see picture below.

Frances was one of the mail carriers in Canterbury, the first woman to do so in Connecticut, and she also had the longest mail route in the state, driving sixty miles every day. She faithfully delivered mail all through her working life, adding both income and interesting news to her family. According to some friends, she also had a good sense for business and played important roles in Eddie's various businesses.

Eddie worked for a paving company for several years, then went into business for himself, building his own oiling truck using a Diamond T cab over and spare parts, including a 4 cylinder Chevy engine to power the oil distributor. As time went on, he added more trucks and men, having seven employees at the height of his gravel hauling and paving business.

In 1951 Ed was diagnosed with Tuberculosis and spent a year in Uncas-on-the-Thames hospital. He was incapacitated personally, but was able to get someone to drive his truck, which was hired out to the town, and Frances took up the slack at home.

At this time, she had her sixty-mile mail route as well as a new baby. As soon as she finished her mail delivery she would go down to visit Ed in the hospital, take him clean clothes and help him in any way she could. Then she would rush back to pick up her baby from the neighbor who watched her during the day. It was a difficult year, but their determination carried them through.

After recovering from TB, Ed got interested in swamp sleds, a kind of boat with a flat hull and an airplane propeller to power it through shallow water in a swamp.

In 1953, he bought a brand-new Ford F600 dump truck from Delany Motors in Central Village for his paving business, and sometime after loaded his air boat and supplies on a trailer, hitched it to his Ford truck and drove it to Florida and back.

It was difficult enough to drive a car down Route 1 in those "pre-Route 95 days," but to do that with a dump truck, navigating through all those cities with all those stop lights was quite a feat.

On the way down, when he reached Virginia, the truck began to backfire. Eddie pulled off to the side of the road, took off the distributor cap and cleaned off the contacts, put it back on and it ran fine—not only on the rest of the trip, but all the way to the next summer.

Along with boats, Ed and Franny had two more children. In spite of his busy life, Ed made time for them. His daughter told how when she came home from school with a project about heating, her father sat down and explained in detail how a hot water heating system worked, including drawing pictures for her. In the picture on left, Ed poses with his two youngest.

Whatever Eddie did, he did well, as can be seen by the driveway on the Wibberley farm, which Eddie paved over 50 years ago and it's still in usable shape.

Since Eddie and my father, Max, were friends, we saw him often. As I remember him, there are two words that come to mind: gracious and ingenious. He was always pleasant and even his wife said she only remembers a couple of times when he was really angry.

One time he came into our tire shop with a tire road hazard problem. The company's guarantee did not cover much; unlike other customers who would get angry at such news, Eddie just quietly and calmly talked it out with Dad, coming to a solution they both could accept. That's the way he was.

In doing paving for a particularly cantankerous customer, one of Eddie's workers complained about the grief the customer was giving them. Eddie's reply was, "Well, that crabby old man is the one who's paying your wages!"

Denis Yarworski told a story illustrating another side of Eddie, his humility and willingness to learn. While helping Eddie change the bucket on a backhoe, Denis suggested a short cut, which Eddie rejected. But the next morning he came to Denis and said that his idea was actually better than the way Eddie wanted to do it and apologized for rejecting it at the moment. Not every boss will do that.

Mechanically Eddie did some astounding things. The one that stands out the most to me was the low bed truck and trailer he built. He transformed an old Diamond T cab-over truck into a front wheel drive system, long before front wheel drive vehicles were even on the market. Then he eliminated the back wheels of the truck and attached the trailer to the

truck so that the wheels of the trailer served as the rear wheels of the truck. People were consistently flummoxed when they saw it. "Where are the rear wheels?" they'd ask, and Eddie would just smile. That trailer, according to Dennis Yaworski, is still up at the town garage.

He took an old Borg Warner car and cut it in half, shortened it and welded it back together, making a cute little vehicle for his son Mike to drive around. It was very popular with his friends.

After years of paving, Eddie decided to try building. His first venture was the professional building on route 169 south of the green, the site of today's Cat Hospital. The impetus for building was so Dr. Frederick, the dentist, could have an office in town. Frances said Eddie would turn in his grave if he knew that his prize building was the cat hospital, as Eddie had no love for cats. This project was followed by building several houses on Elmdale road.

In between Eddie found time to serve two terms as second selectman for Canterbury where he put his practical  genius to work for the good of all. He also served 6 years on the Board of Education, a position which allowed him to present grammar school diplomas to each of his three children, pictured above, right to left: Mary, Linda and Mike.

 Eddie and Frances bought a nice piece of land in Lisbon and when they showed it to Lew Grey and his family, young Lew said, "This would make a great camp ground." So, Eddie and Frances decided to follow that suggestion, in spite of Eddie's statement that he wouldn't "know a camper from a woodchuck!"

They were able to find a banker who was a camper, got a loan and opened the place shortly thereafter. They had a sign which said, "Only 1500 miles from Miami Beach!"

In the beginning, when the camp was small, they were able to visit with all the campers and met lots of interesting people. But as the business grew, they didn't have time to visit. Eddie and Frances lived in the back of the camp store and were constantly busy with both the demands of the business and Eddie's plans for expansion.

In the picture on left are Mike and Ed at the camp ground.

Mike brought his little car there and was a great hit with all the kids who wanted to ride with him.

All three of their children worked at the camp ground and learned to deal with all kinds of people and situations. When confronted with a camper who didn't want to conform and asked, "Why do I have to do this?", the children's answer was, "Because my mother said so!" That ended the argument.

Eddie continued with his paving business on the side during in the Spring and Fall when there were fewer campers, and his son, Mike, worked with him in this.

As he got older, Ed's hearing failed, but he resisted getting hearing aids. However, when he finally did get some, he was amazed to hear again all the birds singing. Shortly after getting them, he lost one while mowing the lawn, but

miraculously found it lying there on the grass when he went to search for it!

After they sold the camp ground, Ed and Frances both wanted to travel, but Frances did not want to camp. In the end, they bought a large van camper and visited every state but Hawaii, and Eddie said if there'd been a road there, he would have gone. Left is a picture of Ed at the Grand Canyon.

He would not consider sailing after the traumatic voyage he'd had on a troop ship returning from his military service in the Pacific; they'd gone through more than one great storm and he'd had enough of ships!

Ed passed away in 2006; Frances at 95 still drives, gardens and is doing well.

Ed and Frances' three children, Mary, Linda and Mike, were all, like their parents, creative and interesting people. Sadly Mary, who had become an oncology nurse, died of melanoma when she was 38. Both Mike and Linda married, and as of 2016 Frances has 11 great grandchildren. Mike, in the picture to the right, works as a helicopter pilot, at present flying for an airline in Afghanistan.

Frances Vaclavik.
--by Sheila

When I grew up in Canterbury on the far end of North Society Road, I thought everyone had a "mail lady" like ours, Frances Vaclavik. What I didn't know, at the time, is that our mail lady was the first woman mail carrier in Connecticut.

Frances' grandfather, Edward Lovell, was a book publisher in New York and his dream was to have a farm in Connecticut. So, when he retired, he moved to Canterbury to become a farmer.

His son, Ralph (Frances' father), came home from WW I to help his father for one year, but he never left. Frances and her sister and two brothers grew up in Canterbury and attended the one-room schoolhouse on the Green.

Frances began work as a mail carrier in 1942 when it cost three cents to mail a letter and one cent for a postcard. She drove 28 miles (12 were on dirt roads) to deliver mail to every house in Canterbury. The post office was in the former

Bennett house just north of the intersection of Route 14 and Route 169, and consisted of two rooms and a closet.

The Mail Carriers Association didn't have a formal meeting place in 1942, so they met in various members' homes. It was at one of these meetings that Frances learned she had the distinction of being the first woman mail carrier in Connecticut.

When the meetings took place, the men would meet in the living room and their wives would gather in the kitchen. When Frances came on the scene, she recalls the ladies craning their necks to get a look at this young twenty-year old stepping into a man's domain. One older Canterbury woman was overheard to say, "it's a man's world and she won't last a year!" They never thought she was "strong enough" for the job, but they were wrong, as she was a mail carrier for thirty years.

Times were different then and Frances went beyond the call of duty in her job. She tells of a house bound elderly woman who lived on Gooseneck Hill Road that would leave, not only her mail in her mailbox, but also her grocery list and Frances would pick up her groceries and deliver them along with her mail the next day.

At Christmas time, she would help parents keep Christmas presents a surprise for children. When large items like skis and sleds arrived, she would hold them at the post office and then deliver them on Christmas morning. This is an example of what our elders refer to as the "good ol' days."

There were touching moments too, like opening P.B. Smith's mailbox on a hot August afternoon and finding a cool glass of homemade root beer that Jean Smith had left for her.

Also, Joe Kulaga, who lived on Water Street, always told her that if she ever got stuck in the mud or snow, just give him a call and he would use his tractor to pull her out.

Another family told her where their house key was, in case she ever needed to use the phone. She also knew Dr. Helen Baldwin, who would often be waiting by the mailbox with her sister, Lucy, when Frances arrived, waiting for her N.Y. Times, which Frances often used as a bee swatter. The reason she had bees in her car was because bee hives, along

with little chickens and ducks were all delivered by mail and there were sometimes a few runways.

Along with her busy life as a mail carrier, mother and helper in her husband's paving business, Frances took time for her gardening, especially raising flowers. In order to extend her growing season, Ed built her a green house on the side of their house (see picture below).

In 1956, Frances took some time off to have her third child. By this time there were sixty miles of road in Canterbury and the substitute driver couldn't complete the route as quickly as Frances could. This greatly

disturbed the many dairy and egg farmers in Canterbury that did not get their checks in time to get to the bank by 3:00pm.

So, Priscilla Botti circulated a petition to create two routes in Canterbury. The postal service agreed and Frances only had to deliver to half of Canterbury and Addison Davis did the other half.

When Frances retired in 1972, she devoted more time to her husband Ed, her children and grandchildren and her gardens. Her flower gardens are breathtaking and just a walk through them makes you appreciate her hard work as well as her love of beauty and nature.

I'll always think of Frances Vaclavik as my mail lady, but she is really an example of conscientious and caring public servant who went out of her way to help the people on her mail route.

105

Eleanor Orlomoski   --by Sheila Mason Gale

It's just not Christmas in Canterbury until the decorations go up on the hill at the intersection of Route 169 and Bennett Pond Road. Alton and Eleanor Orlomoski created and continue this Canterbury Christmas tradition.

In 1908, Eleanor's Grandparents, Truman and Maude Hart, moved from Southington, Connecticut to

Canterbury and bought the colonial house just north of Quinebaug Valley Farm on 169. As a matter of fact, Eleanor and her sister Nancy were born in that house.

Her grandfather Truman was a motorman on a trolley in Southington and Eleanor's father, Charles, remembers traveling to Canterbury on a trolley when he was a child. Charles was the oldest of nine children and he grew up in that house.

As an adult, Charles worked in textile mills in the area and this is where he met his wife, Hilda. After they married, they rented the house on the west side of Ed's Garage and started a family. You may know their children, Kenneth Hart, Arthur Hart, Marjorie Orlomoski, Eleanor Orlomoski, Nancy Allyn and William Hart.

They rented from Fremont Smith from 1936 to 1953 at $7.00/month. Fremont's father was George Washington Smith, who was the owner of a hoop shop and blacksmith shop directly across the road from the house.

Hoops made there were to hold the sails to the masts of a ship. Eleanor and her sisters and brothers were allowed to play in the hoop shop, but not when

106

they used steam to bend the hoops. That would have been too dangerous.

When Eleanor was a child, she and her siblings felt very safe in town and walked everywhere. They were allowed to walk to the Canterbury Green from their house and enjoyed visiting the Library (next to where Calvary Chapel is today) and would walk home with an armload of books. They would get their  fishing poles and head out to Kitt Brook or a fishing hole on Elmdale Road and spend the day. On the left is Elenor's sixth grade picture.

She remembers taking some peanut butter and crackers and hiking over to the property across the street from their house to sit under the cool pines.

Her brothers would ride their bikes all over Canterbury and even to Plainfield. In the winter, they would put their sleds in the middle of the road, starting just above her house and slide all the way down to the Bacon Bridge just before Plainfield. Lovell Lane was a dirt road then and hardly any traffic went in or out of Canterbury.

There were no other children in the neighborhood, so siblings were their only playmates. They went to square dances at the Grange Hall (where the VFW is today) and the Volunteer Fire Company would bring minstrel shows to Canterbury as an annual fund raiser.

When she was a child, Mr. Robinson lived in the Prudence Crandall house and he had a big garden in the lot where Ed's Garage is today.

Eleanor went to first grade at the Frost School and then the Green School for second and third grade. She next attended fourth grade in the Baldwin one room schoolhouse on Route 169 (almost across the street from Gooseneck Hill Road). For fifth grade she went to Frost School and then when Dr. Helen Baldwin School was built, she completed grades six, seven and eight.

Muriel Carter was her favorite teacher. Ms. Carter played the accordion and the children would march around the Green to her music. She encouraged every child to learn to play the recorder and she created a Xylophone-type instrument made from glass tubes, which the children would play with wooden sticks.

Eleanor went to Griswold High School where some of her schoolmates were Allyn Tracy Woods, Bob Romanoff, Bob Grab, Ronny Fault, Barbara Dombrowski and Emerson Reynolds. She graduated third in her class, but, unfortunately, there was no money to go to college, so she looked for a job.

Eleanor was involved in 4-H and, like many of us, she was taught by Elsie Hawes. For spending money she and her sisters would clean Elsie's house and be paid $3.00, maybe up to $5.00. She felt "rich" when she got $5.00!

Elsie worked as a clerk in the post office, and since it

 wasn't very busy, she would allow Eleanor to come to the post office where she taught her how to knit. Elsie and Addison Davis were later influential in helping Eleanor get a job at the post office.

She started as a clerk (in picture above) and in1962 she became a full-time rural mail carrier after Frances Vaclavik retired. She worked six days a week and said it was an interesting job.

When she started ,there was no UPS or Fed Ex, so the mail was the only way to send items such as tires, baby chicks, and even urns with ashes. Below is Eleanor on her last day of mail delivery before she retired in 1992 after 30 years of service.

When Eleanor was young, the Swan family owned the filling station where Bergeron's Garage is located today. In those days, Swan's was well known for their ice cream, which they sold for five cents a scoop. One day when Mrs. Swan was dishing out ice cream, she asked if Eleanor would pump gas for a customer who had driven in.

The customer was Alton Orlomoski who had recently moved with his parents to Quinebaug Valley Farm where his stepfather was the herdsman. This chance meeting started a friendship. She said he was always fun and had a story to tell.

She still enjoys his company and finds him fun because in the following year, 1955, she married Alton and in 1956 her sister Marjorie married Alton's brother Kendall.

Alton and Eleanor bought the hill property on Bennett Pond Road from the Swans and raised three children there–

Steven, David and Amy. David lives in Colebrook, while Steve and Amy live in Canterbury.

Her son Steve was a member of the Canterbury Historical Society and he told Eleanor and Alton he would pay for their membership the first year if they wanted to join. She and Alton have since been very active in the Historical Society and especially the Green School restoration.

Since she was born and lived in town all her life, Eleanor finds the history of the town fascinating and enjoys studying all aspects of Canterbury's history. She said Canterbury is a more modern town now.

In the early forties, there were probably only about 1,000 people in town and lots were chicken farmers and some dairy farmers. She can remember cans of milk being hauled down to the railroad depot in South Canterbury to be sent off to market. But all that is gone, now

Eleanor always loved Christmas and so when she and Alton had their own home, they decided to put up Christmas decorations on the lawn. Her son, David, made the first reindeer that appeared on the hill.

The family has been doing this for a long time and Eleanor mentioned to her family that maybe it was time to stop putting up the decorations. Her daughter and granddaughters said, "No!" and that they would be glad to help in any way to keep the Christmas decorations on the hill. Thanks to the Orlomoski family for this Canterbury tradition.

Alton Orlomoski 1929
--by Steve

Al grew up in Willimantic, being the second oldest of four; he's right in the middle of the picture above. He left home at 16 to join the Merchant Marine (picture on left). But after a short time of training, he decided he wasn't cut out to be a sailor. He was seasick a lot, and he said that when you're seasick, at first you're afraid the ship will sink, then you hope it will.

In 1946 he joined the army for 3 years, signing up for the cavalry because, he said, it's better than walking. He also asked to be assigned to the Pacific (as opposed to Panama or Alaska) and ended up in Japan.

He was trained on
machineguns (on right) and
mortars.

His company
provided security for
the embassy and he
personally guarded General MacArthur.

The paratroopers from 11th airborne
gave him a hard time
because he wore
paratrooper boots, so he
asked to be transferred to
11th airborne, and went to jump school
(jumping out of the plane in picture on
right). He was trained as a gunner on
an 81 millimeter mortar in a heavy
weapons unit. When he got out after his three tour, he
spent three more years in the active reserves.

In 1953, when he was living for a time with his
parents, his step father got a job as a herdsman on
Quinnebaug valley farm in Canterbury, so Al moved with
them.

As Eleanor told in her story, they met at Swan's gas
station in 1954, then married in 1955. Eleanor was just
out of high school and only 18, while Al was 25 with lots of
experience, so her mother thought he was too old for her.
But, as Eleanor said recently, "Here we are 62 years later
and our marriage is going well!"

When they married, Al was working as a mechanic
at Wright's tractor service in Willimantic. This was
followed by a series of interesting jobs. For three years he
was a Willimantic police man, then he ran a back hoe and
bulldozer for a contractor. After that he worked for the
State as a truck driver, hauling heavy equipment. He also
mowed along 395 in the summers, going all the way from
Occum to Mass line and back. After he retired, an
administrator from Dr. Helen Baldwin called Al and asked

if he could fill in as a custodian for a week; he ended up staying for 10 years.

Al has been a trapper for much of his life, starting when he was 12, living in Willimantic near the Natchaug river. He got interested one day after seeing a man who had caught a muskrat. In the beginning Al trapped mostly skunks, selling them to a neighbor who skinned them. He got the amazing price of $1.50 per skin, quite a sum for a boy in 1941. To give you an idea of the economy of the time, Al said it only cost 12 cents to go to the movies.

Al's teacher wasn't too happy with his trapping, though, as Al often smelled like skunk when he came to school. She would send him home, telling him to come back when he smelled better. Al said he didn't mind at all!

Other than the time he was in the service, Al

continued to trap for the next 50 years. He caught muskrat, raccoon, mink, otter and beaver. Most of the 150 beaver he caught were for local towns. Beavers would build dams that flooded roads or caused other problems, and if the town crews cleared out the dam, within a short time the beavers would build another one. So, the only real solution was to trap them. In the picture to the left Al holds the skin of the biggest beaver he ever caught. On the right is a picture of "stretching boards" for curing skins.

I asked Al about trapping foxes, but he said it was illegal and he only once caught a fox by mistake in a muskrat trap.

Al has a nice collection of skins, ranging from a weasel up to a black bear, which he takes to local schools where the kids like to stroke the furs.

Al said he no longer trapped, but when he took me to the cellar to see his collections, he found he'd caught a mouse in a trap there!

Speaking of collections, Al is a collector of many things. When he first moved to Canterbury in 1953, his neighbor, Milo Appely, got him interested in collecting arrowheads by showing him his collection.

Since Al lived on Quinnebaug farm right next to the river where the Indians had camped, he found lots of artifacts in the corn fields. He also found many in the Moosup Pond area and near the Danielson Sewer Treatment site which used to be an Indian campsite. He has a collection of about 450 artifacts, some pictured above.

Al has a large collection of traps, including 40 bear traps (see pictures on next page). His specialty is hand-forged, blacksmith-made traps. He has an affinity for blacksmith work because his grandfather was a blacksmith in Scotland.

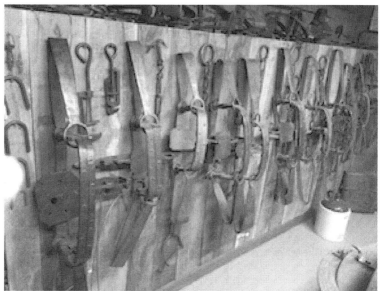

Above are some of his fearsome bear traps

The traps in the foreground were made in Germany.

The traps above are handmade ones.

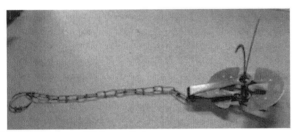

The trap here was patented in Willimantic. There are only eight of these traps still in existence

He also collects stoneware, called salt glazed

pottery, shown here. He started by buying one made in the early 1800s in Norwich. He said that Norwich had eight or nine active potteries, the best known being Mr. Risely's, who produced his pottery from 1846 to 1881. There were other active pottery kilns in New London and Hartford, so Al has some products from them as well.

Another interest of his is decoys, and of course, he has a collection of these.

And then there is his collection of milk bottles.

More importantly, Al also collected friends and had a special service to older people, visiting them when they were sick and incapacitated, faithfully seeing them until they died.

Al is an active reader and since he has three librarians in his family, is amply supplied with books of his interests. At 88 Al is still fit and strong. The day I came to interview him, he'd been out to buy plants for the garden and then was working on replacing boards in his porch floor. May he live long and continue to contribute to the lives of others in Canterbury and beyond.

Frank Strmiska 1930-2015
--by Steve

Frank was of Czech background, born and raised in Norwalk, CT. That's him and his sister in this picture. His father had relatives in Canterbury, being a brother to Theresa Gallegher, and Ed Vaclavik being an uncle to Frank, so they visited here often where Frank, at times, worked for Ed.

Frank and his uncle Ed were a lot alike, being very interested in machines, creative in building things and

enjoying working hard. This relationship encouraged Frank to move to Canterbury in 1960 with his wife (in their wedding picture on left) and seven children, two girls and five boys: Dave, the twins Cindy and Jim, Jeff, Sherry, Pete and Tim.

He bought a house from Ed Vac, in the picture below. It is across the street from the

present Strmiska garage on Route 14, just below the Green (junction of 14 and 169).

Eventually Frank's father bought a farm in Brooklyn and Frank's boys often helped their grandfather there. With their father being so busy with work, the boys spent more time with their grandfather than Frank.

Frank's father, being a mason, decided to put a cellar under Frank's house and went to work, digging it out by hand with a shovel and wheelbarrow, building a stone foundation for it as he went. Like most people who had lived through the depression, Frank's father knew how to do things without the proper tools and, like a typical Strmiska, he could see a need

118

and meet it, even if it all had to be done by hand.

As Frank went into business, he joined a number of other contractors living and working in Canterbury, among them Cliff Williams, Art Grab, Ted Dean Sr, the Swan boys, and Ed Vac. They all were friends, in spite of being competitors, and often helped each other, even hiring one another to finish jobs.

Frank started by buying an old Fordson Major tractor with a backhoe and did excavation work. He dug dry wells, foundations, did grading, septic systems, driveways and whatever else came along. He also did a lot of road building in Canterbury and surrounding towns. He wasn't afraid to take on big jobs; he just figured out how to get them done.

Work in those days was much more difficult than

today. There were no four-wheel drives, no cabs, no heat or air conditioning on the machines, no ability to work in really muddy conditions, like in this picture.

As Frank bought other equipment, he did a lot of jury rigging on his tractors to make them more useful and durable, brazing broken parts, taking out piston sleeves, putting in oversized pistons, replacing engines, ever seeking to make the work go better.

As time went on, Frank saw ways to modify his equipment to meet the demands of his expanding business, and he proceeded to alter or invent things long before others thought of them.

For instance, he made a hydraulic thumb for his backhoe bucket (see picture on right). Up to that time there were only hand operated thumbs which were clumsy and time consuming to use. His invention was so effective that

the Ackerman representative came out to take pictures of it, and used the idea for their machines.

He modified the tailgate of his dump truck so that it could open from the side like a door, or swing from the top like a conventional one. At that time, such a thing could not be bought, although they are available now.

He put together a hydraulic wood splitter, long before such a thing was known; his boys said it was crude but effective. In the picture to the left, the boys are using it. Note that it is attached to his bulldozer.

He also put a backhoe on his bulldozer, another new idea, modifying it to fit, so when they were doing septic systems, one machine could do all the types of work needed.

He also built his own pump trucks for septic cleaning, and put the pump controls on the back, rather than in the cab,

making it easier for the driver to operate it. At that time, there was no such thing as a pump truck on the market, so Frank, as usual, filled the void. He encouraged his boys and his grandchildren to follow his lead, to use their heads and be creative, too.

Frank would improve on things, while his uncle Ed would "go deeper" and come up with wild ideas, like putting a Pontiac car motor and transmission in a dozer!

Unconventional, but it worked.

Frank didn't buy new equipment often, but when he did, he went for the newest, the state of the art machine, like when he bought a Case dozer with a four-way bucket. No one else had one and he knew that it would give him an edge in bidding, because he could do the job faster than his competition. The Strmiska boys still have that dozer (picture above) for parts.

Frank also thought about having equipment that would last for 20 years. In fact, a number of his machines lasted a lot longer because he kept them up and could fix most anything.

In the 60's he bought a dozer with a six-way blade and a torque converter transmission instead of a conventional clutch, which made it faster, better suited to his work. He had one of the first excavators around, and got a lot of work  burying stonewalls for farmers. Jim said they buried miles of walls; he commented that if the farmers had waited, thy could have sold the stones instead of paying Frank to bury them!

Frank never stuck to one brand; he would buy whatever was good for him. He had Ford, John Deere, Case, Ackerman. Volvo and International machines.

He could weld anything; his boys say it wasn't generally pretty, but it was strong. Frank had lost an eye in an accident while working in a wood shop as a youngster and this hampered him with welding and tasks like grading and digging, so he gladly let his boys or Dad help him in his  work. In this picture you can see Frank squinting with his blind eye in the bright sunlight

 He was the kind of person who know how to figure things out and expected his boys to do the same. He'd give them a job without telling them how to do it, and leave, being sure they'd get it done, like grading off a field as in this picture

121

As the boys grew older, they were drafted by Frank to work in specific areas of the business. Jim became the mechanic, Dave the pump man, Jeff does the bidding and excavating. Pete now works in landscaping for another company, and Tim now works for the town.

His boys said that Frank not only worked hard in his business, he also worked hard on holidays and vacations. Thanksgiving Day for Frank was a time to cut firewood. In fact, with his boys helping, and using Franks' hydraulic splitter, they could cut and split enough wood in one day to last for the whole winter. Thanksgiving dinner didn't come until evening for them!

Frank loved to fish; it was his passion. He always had a boat and went fishing whenever he could. He even tried his hand at lobstering for a while.

He liked to go to Florida in the winter for open ocean saltwater fishing—the further out the better. Even on vacation with Frank there was no lolling around in the boat, everyone had to have at least one line in the water, preferably two. Frank would want to go home with a catch of 200 or more fish and he wanted everyone to contribute. Let's get with it!

However, as Frank saw the decline in the number of fish in the ocean, he switched to catch and release, wanting future generations to be able to fish, too.

In his later years, Frank came down with Parkinson's and he eventually had to withdraw from active work in the business, giving full responsibility to his boys.

He enjoyed his grandchildren, in this picture holding Jared, as well as reading western novels, but in the end couldn't even do that. I (Steve) visited him several times when he was confined to a chair; I was sad to see him, like my father, Max, unable to get about after having lived such an active life. But this will come to all of us.

Frank died in 2015 at age 85, leaving a living legacy in his boys who carry on his vision of working creatively out of their building just below the Green.

If you watch, you'll see the Strmiska boys around town, hauling gravel with what was Frank's truck.

Gloria Coombs
--by Sheila

When I (Sheila) was eleven, I would often go horseback riding with Linda Bassett. We would ride along Water Street and always rode next door to the Coombs farm. I remember wishing I could ride a horse like Gloria Coombs Scharlack. She was so at ease and comfortable in the saddle.

I recently met with Gloria and her cousin Edward Chartier to talk about the Coombs family. In 1911 George Coombs and his wife Laura Coombs moved to Canterbury from New Jersey and bought a 135 acre (more or less) farm. They had six children: Harvey, Roger, Helen, Elsie, George and Charles.

Helen married Edward Chartier and had two children: Laura and Edward.

Elsie married Harold Chartier and they had six children: Gertrude, Harold, Lillian, Arlene, Shirley and Harry.

George joined the service and moved to California.

Charles married Mildred Slater and they had eight children: Eugene, Phyllis, Theodore, Fred, Helen, Raymond, Elaine and Judy.

Charles was one of the men who helped construct Butts Bridge and I'm sure many of you know his son, Ray  Coombs, Sr. who is involved in many Canterbury activities.

The farm was large and was on both sides of Water Street. It was eventually divided into two farms. Roger ran the original homestead on Water Street, pictured here, and Harvey ran one on Cemetery Road. Roger and Ethel had three children, Richard, Clifford and Gloria. Harvey and Sadie had four children, George, Irene, Julia and Estelle. Harvey later married Dorothy and had one son, Robert.

Many of you might remember Harvey's son George Coombs who was a school bus driver and was also the Road Crew Foreman for Town of Canterbury for many years. He built the original town garage on Kinne Road. I wish I could have interviewed George about his life in Canterbury because he was a great storyteller. He would sometimes tell me stories about the time he served in the military. Just a few years ago George won the award for being the most decorated living WW II veteran.

As a child, Gloria remembers a quiet neighborhood. Some of her neighbors were the Bassetts, Bullards, Pattersons, Lachapells and the Papugas who had the country store at the end of Water Street.

Gloria's brothers, Richard and Cliff, went to the Gayhead School, while Gloria went to the Westminster school for three years until the Dr. Helen Baldwin School opened.

Farming was a hard life and the whole family had to pitch in to help, but there was time for fun too. The Coombs children and neighbors would get together and go bicycle riding and horseback riding. There were plenty of open fields where they played baseball. It was easy to get a team together once the Bassetts moved into the neighborhood, because they had eight children.

In the summer, they would go over to Ted Dean's house and go swimming. Mr. Dean even put an old bus out by the pond for changing their clothes. Gloria and her friend, Ruth Bassett, would go horseback riding around Canterbury and even rode over to Scotland.

As they got older, they would go square dancing on Saturday nights or to the movies. This was in the 1950's when it only cost 25 cents to see a movie and a pint of ice cream cost 10 cents. Also, there were the young people's activities at Westminster Church and Calvary Chapel.

Gloria went to Griswold High School where other students would often tease her by asking if she got there by stagecoach. I remember the same joke because the kids used to say the same thing to me a decade later.

When George Coombs decided to retire as a school bus driver in 1967, he asked Gloria if she wanted to take his position. She talked it over with her husband, Bob, and said, "Yes." She has been doing it ever since.

There is quite a Coombs family history of caring for Canterbury school age children because not only did George and Gloria drive school bus, but her brother Richard drove buses for 53 years. I think that is a record.

She tells of the time she was driving the bus and a boy had a several books of matches in his back pocket. When he sat down they scraped against the seat, ignited and set his coat on fire. He jumped out of the bus with Gloria on his heels telling him to roll in the snow.

Over her many years of driving, Gloria said she has come to the conclusion that the kids in Canterbury are good, decent children.

Four or five generations of the original Coombs family (George and Laura) still live in Canterbury. A few of the families the Coombs have married into are the Bassetts, Millers, Thurlows, Chartiers and Gallagers.

The original farm is now owned by Richard and Phyllis Bassett Coombs. They run it with their sons Richard, Kenneth and Jesse and their daughter Debbie Leone handles the bookkeeping.

Canterbury was built on farming and it is good to see the Coombs family keeping it alive and going strong. George and Laura Coombs would be very proud of the legacy they left their children and Canterbury.

Henry Strube 1917-1997
--by Steve

REV. HENRY STRUBE

Reverend Henry Strube had connections with Canterbury long before he moved here in 1951. He and his wife, Lois, were missionaries working in Columbia, South America in the 1940s. As they were supported by Calvary Chapel, they visited Canterbury each time they came to the US.

Mr. Strube was full of fun and life. He liked to tell jokes and had some he told a lot, like how he asked his wife to marry him. "I said to her, 'Wilt thou marry me?' and she wilted." And about his first night living in the jungles of Columbia. They stayed in a

thatched roof hut and after getting into bed, creatures began to fall from the rafters onto the bed. He said he wasn't sure what all of them were, beyond rats, lizards and a snake or two, but as each one fell, he'd hit it with a stick and throw it on the floor.

In one rainy season when they were living in the jungle, their oldest child became ill. Since the roads were impassable because of the deep mud, they were unable to get the boy out for medical care, and he died.

It was, of course, a tragic happening and they mourned the boy's death. But Pastor Strube said that the Indians attitude towards them changed much to the positive after that, as they saw how the Strubes were willing to live and lose as they did.

After they moved to a ministry in an urban center, Pastor Strube survived three assassination attempts. In one incident, his whole family was fed food containing ground glass, but miraculously they were not injured.

Later when Pastor Strube was preaching on the street, a mob came after him. He was able to get into his truck, but they surrounded him and turned the truck over, hoping to kill hime, but only succeeded in cutting off two of his fingers.

Another time he was in his kitchen moving the galvanized container they used for a bath tub. Just when he bent over to move it, a bullet came in the open window and went right through his hair. Later the gunman became a follower of Jesus and told Pastor Strube that the local religious leader had promised to marry him for free if he killed Mr. Strube!

In 1951 the Strubes returned to live in the US, bringing  their three children with them, Harold, Pricilla and Lois. Calvary Chapel was in need of a pastor, so they asked Pastor Strube to come take the position,.

He and Mrs. Strube were real work horses, serving the congregation in many ways. He said he was always ready to preach, pray or die at a moment's notice. For him every part of that saying was true.

 In the church Mr. Strube taught Sunday School, preached the sermon both Sunday morning and evening, taught at prayer meeting and any other time there was an opportunity.

He liked to tell how he prepared his sermons at night, always keeping a 22. rifle on the desk so he could shoot the rats that came out of the baseboards of the old parsonage. In his time the parsonage was the house next to Creative Interiors.

He was very interested in meeting people where they were in life, as willing to help folks get in hay, milk a cow or take them to the hospital as he was to preach, teach a class or visit the sick. He was also a good mechanic, fixing his own car and anyone else's that needed work.

In interviewing people about him, one word they used a lot to describe him was "fun." He and his wife led the youth group and he was always finding a new place to take them. Claire Ellston remembers how entertaining their times were in the "Young Peoples" group with Pastor Strube: swimming, ice skating, roller skating, trips to the beach and to camp.

He bought an old hearse to take the young people to events, including Word of Life Camp in Schroon Lake in NY. More than once that "re-hearse" broke down on the road, but with Mr. Strube along, they always got it running again.

Pastor Strube set up a program for the young people whereby they could earn a scholarship to attend Word of Life Camp by memorizing Bible verses.

Claire also recalled that she and Mary Eastland would go every Sunday afternoon with the Strubes to sing in special services. One week they would go to convalescent homes in Plainfield, the next to one in Brooklyn and also the jail there. Pastor Strube, of course, always had a message ready to give.

He was a real evangelist, wanting to share the joy and goodness of his faith with everyone. He put up signs on the hill by Little River, so when people drove up it going East,

  they could clearly read the good news.

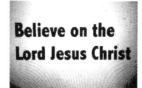 

He was also a match maker. Don Woods recounted how, when he first came to Canterbury to get to know Allyn

Tracey, he stayed the night at the Strubes, and before getting to bed, Pastor Strube asked him, "Are you going to marry her?" Don was shocked as he wasn't quite ready for such a commitment at that point!

As attendance grew under his leadership, the church put on an addition. Mr. Strube, of course, was right in there swinging a hammer and wielding a paint brush.

Then in the early morning of March 24, 1954 a fire broke out in the church, and by the time the fire company got there, the building was engulfed in flames. Mr. Strube arrived at the same time, having thrown on his clothes over his pajamas. He rushed into the foyer of the church and rescued the offering box for the addition. In the end, all expect the front wall of the church burned, including the new addition that had just been completed.

The reporter for the Norwich Bulletin came over to Mr. Strube and said, "Well, I guess that's the end of your work here in Canterbury!"

"Oh no," Pastor Strube replied, "This is only the beginning. God is telling us that our addition was too small! We're going to build bigger and better!"

When the fire company was done with their work, the chief, Merritt Hawes, came over to Pastor Strube and apologized that they hadn't been able to do more. Then he added, "Why don't you put that offering box out here in front of the church, so people coming to look at the remains can give something, if they want."

Mr. Strube liked that idea and set it up. Many people came to see the church burn, and then the ruins; many also put a contribution in the box. Mr. Stube kept that box out there for weeks, and emptied it every day. In the end, enough was given to complete the cellar and cap it.

Following the fire, the church used the old Town Hall Annex next door to meet in, and held Sunday School classes in cars and the parsonage during the summer.

By October the new foundation had been completed and weather proofed, so the church could begin meeting there. The upper structure, made of fire proof lava blocks, was built quickly and the church was able to begin using it in February of 1957.

The Strubes served in Canterbury until 1961 when they moved to Florida to work with Spanish speaking migrant workers.

Mr. Strube, as always, was practical and frugal in his work. He told me he'd look for an old Pontiac with more than 100,000 miles on it, buy it cheaply, change the motor oil and transmission fluid, then drive it for 100,000 more miles across those flat open stretches of Florida.

Every night he visited several migrant work camps. He would gather the hundreds of men who worked there, sing songs, preach a sermon in Spanish, and sometimes show a film.

He always explained the gospel, the need we all have for a Savior and how Jesus died to pay the penalty for our sins, and rose from the dead to buy us eternal life. He always made clear the need for making a personal decision to accept Christ as one's own Savior and Lord. Many listeners made that decision over the years.

My father, Max, visited the Strubes in Florida several times and would accompany Mr. Strube on his evening outreaches. Dad would play his trumpet and the men would gather, first to hear him play, and then to listen to Mr. Stube speak

131

During the day, Mr. Strube worked as a "shopper" for missionaries working in South America. They would send requests for goods not available there and he would find them at a good price, buy and ship them out. He also collected lots of "reject vegetables" (ones that were too large or too small) from the canning factories, and distributed them to the needy in the area.

In the end, Mr. Strube returned to Canterbury. He died in Florida in 1997, was cremated and his ashes were sent to Canterbury where is buried in the cemetery behind Calvary Chapel.

Helen Baldwin, M.D. 1865-1946
--by Steve

Dr. Helen Baldwin's family first moved to Canterbury when
Benjamin Baldwin settled here in 1704. Helen was born 161

years later in Canterbury, on
November 14, 1865, the daughter of
Dr. Elijah Baldwin Jr. and Sarah
(Mathewson) Baldwin.

She began her education in
the one room Baldwin School in the
Southern part of the town and went
on to become a well-known doctor
and surgeon, an unusual feat for a
woman in her time. She was a
remarkable woman, a tireless worker,
a pioneer in many ways and a "Canterburian" all her life.

An article about her, written by a fellow doctor, was
printed in the *The Medical World Magazine* in December,
1940. As this was the only extensive source of information I
could find on Dr. Baldwin, who died the year I was born, the
full article is reprinted beginning beginning here.

There are people who have an indefinable something,
which destines them to stand out amongst their

contemporaries. Such a
human being is Dr. Helen
Baldwin. She seems
always to have good
judgment, every
experience teaching her
something to add to her
value, and making her,
through her entire career,
seemingly wise beyond
her years. [In picture on
the left we see young
Helen with her sister
Lucy.]

133

She received an AB degree from Wellesley College in 1888 with a special certificate in physics and chemistry. The next year she served on the faculty at Wellesley as laboratory demonstrator in physics.

She came to the New York Infirmary Medical School in her junior year, having left Ann Arbor because of the better clinical facilities in a large city.

She graduated in 1892 and took an internship in the New England Hospital for Women and Children, and after completion of this service, she felt the need for further preparation before entering private practice. So, she decided, in 1893, to join the Post-Graduate group at Johns Hopkins. Thus, she became one of the first women working under the galaxy of famous physicians, Osler, Welsh, Kelly and Halstead, who were making American medical history. She repeatedly said that here she received the inspiration for research, which for years she continued, parallel with her practice.

Her next step was the examination for the Philadelphia General Hospital, which appointment she received and remained there two years.)

On returning to New York in 1896, she identified herself with the New York Infirmary for Women and Children, at first teaching in the Women's Medical College of the Infirmary as assistant in Clinical Medicine and Instructor in Physiology from 1896-1900, when the college closed.

Then she served in the medical department of the hospital for 40 years as clinician, junior attending, head of department and finally as consultant.

It is impossible for her contemporaries to appreciate in full her influence as a physician and person. Through the years, a large number of younger doctors were taught by her, in her department, each and every one felt the contact with Dr. Baldwin a privilege.

She, in turn, made it plain that she thought the continuous contact with fresh young minds stimulating for her own growth. With her contemporaries, she served on all the  important hospital committees and gave us increasing constructive aid.

During these forty years, Dr. Baldwin also built up and conducted an active private practice. In addition, for sixteen years, 1896 to 1912, she worked in pathological chemistry in the laboratory of Dr. Christian Herter, one of the pioneers in biochemistry. In1905 she worked as an expert in chemistry under the referee board of the US Department of Agriculture.

She published a number of scientific articles in the medical journals, some purely experimental in character, others clinical. Thus from 1897 to 1924 her name appeared at intervals in medical periodicals of the time. [In the picture below, Dr. Baldwin waits in Canterbury for the train to take her back to New York.]

 She retired from many of her activities in the late 1930s, moving to her beloved home town of Canterbury, coming occasionally to NY to care for some of her elderly patients who did not want to be transferred to another doctor.

So valuable did she seem to her town's people that, upon her return to her home town, she was appointed the Health Officer in Canterbury, CT, starting in January 1939

until she passed on to her reward on the 17th of April 1946.

In all of us who have been associated with her, she aroused increasing admiration, because of her high courage and dauntless spirit. During one of her internships she contracted scarlet fever; this affected her hearing and in ten years she grew quite deaf. She surmounted this handicap in an almost miraculous way. This is fully substantiated by her outstanding career—enviable and wholly admirable.

--The Medical World Magazine, December, 1940

Below is a picture of Dr. Helen Baldwin one year before she died. Dr. Baldwin is in the back on the right; in front of her is her sister, Miss Lucy; the others are Mrs. Hadley (with the head covering), another sister of Dr. Baldwin, and Mrs. Hadley's daughter.

James Yaworski 1912-1997
--by Steve

Jim plowing snow in 1947 in Packerville with his son Denis

James Yaworski's parents came from Poland in 1908. Their name was actually spelled "Jaworski," but it was mispronounced so often that Jim changed the spelling to help people say it correctly.

In 1930, at the age of 18, Jim married his sweetheart, Rose, when she was only 14, and they moved from Montville to Canterbury the same year. They had a good marriage, shown by the fact that it lasted for 67 fine years.

After settling in Canterbury, Jim got a job at the Paperboard Corporation, but wanted to do more, so in 1936 he bought a Ford dump truck. Rose would shovel it full of fine sand during the day and when Jim got home for work, he

would deliver the load. They were a good team right from the beginning. In the picture on the left, Jim poses with his truck and young Arnold Greenman, who later had a large trucking and earthmoving company of his own.

Shortly after settling in Canterbury Jim was elected to the selectmen's board in 1935, along with Hans Hansen and Kurt Kinne. It was a responsibility that Jim enjoyed.

These selectmen hired teenagers Newt Bingham, the  Miller boys and Max Wibberley to work on the road crew. They also oversaw the building of Butts Bridge (pictured here; the old bridge can be seen on far left). They were able to get 90% of the cost covered by the state, with Canterbury paying only $10,000. Even with this great savings they were criticized. But they were vindicated in the hurricane of 1955 when there was water 19 feet deep over fields in Packerville. The bridge below the

Green on Route 14 (pictured above) was washed out on the Plainfield side.

Butts Bridge was the only bridge usable from the Mass line to Norwich. As all the traffic in the area had to use Butts Bridge, there was a sign at the end of Packerville Road pointing to Route 12, saying "NYC this way."

In another significant event in 1935, Jim and Rose joined with Lucy Hansen, Vinnie Williams, Pastor Grecian and several others who helped start Calvary Chapel. They wanted to use the old Methodist building on "Canterbury Plains," so Jim went down to NYC to talk with the Methodist

138

Church Board and got permission to take over the building, which, they found was in dire need of repair.

It rained the day of their first service and the roof leaked so badly that they had to put out pots and pans around the sanctuary. Jim said the rain played its own tune in those pots during the sermon.

The original founders were an uneducated bunch, but they drew up a constitution for Calvary Chapel that remains essentially the same eighty-five years later. They may not have been educated, but they were practical and knew their Bible.

Jim was a perfectionist, wanting to do things right, which often meant that he demanded others do things his way or not at all, so he had conflict all his life. But at the same time, he was a peace maker, helping others work out their conflicts.

He continued to work hard, having three jobs for much of his young years. He drove school bus days—and had his own school bus at one time--doing the Kindergarten run; he liked to sing hymns for the kids while he drove. He continued running his trucking and dump business in between, and also worked nights for the Gilman brothers. He looked tired all the time.

At one point he also worked at Electric Boat on the Nautilus submarine. At the launching, he and a fellow worker were the ones to knock out the blocks holding the sub, releasing it to slide down the ramp way into the water. The Captain of the Nautilus came over to shake hands with Jim and his partner (pictured above), saying they were the kind of people that made America function.

In addition to all this, Jim and Rose had a farm with 30 head of dairy cows, all milked by hand, as well as chickens. Rose took care of running the farm while she also raised strawberries and flowers to sell. Her favorites were mums and Iris.

To the left are Jim and Rose in their later years standing with one of their earlier trucks that Dennis restored.

Plastic Film, a company in Plainfield, asked Jim if they could dump their refuse on his land and he agreed. Others, hearing of this agreement, also wanted to take advantage of this possibility, and Jim's landfill business grew, along with his trucking.

In 1958 he wanted to buy a new Tera-Track Loader to keep the landfill leveled. He went to the Jewett City Trust to borrow the money, and when he told the loan officer he wanted $238,000, the officer was so shocked that Jim got up, went around the desk and patted the man on the shoulder saying, "It's alright now." The officer called the bank

president who told him to go ahead and loan the money, as Jim was known as a good and honest businessman.

To the left is a picture of Jim sitting on one of his big dozers.

Jim also bought more trucks to haul waste. One of those later trucks he named "Miss Rose" for his wife. When she asked why it took him so long to name one after her he replied, "I wanted to make sure you were in this for the long haul!"

Jim's sons, Dennis and James II, joined him in the business. James worked with his Dad in the land fill side of things, while Dennis focused on the trucking side. At one point, Dennis had over sixty rigs, some seen in the picture below, hauling ash from the garbage burning plant near Taftville

Denis also started a collection of old trucks, restoring some of them to pristine condition, like the ones below.

Eventually he put them on display in the "Haul of Fame Museum," in Packervill, along with old cars and other

vehicles, including Cliff William's Piper Cub airplane.

Jim and Rose worked hard to the end and died old and full of years, leaving a legacy for Canterbury in their grandchildren.

Rose Yaworski 1916-2008
   --by Sheila

Did you know Canterbury once had a hotel on Packer Road in the 20's? Rose Yaworski remembers Packer Hotel just down the street from the Packer Mill. As a child, she used to play on the massive porch which encircled the entire building.

Both of Rose's parents (John and Magalene Hatt) came individually from Poland and entered America through Ellis Island. They met in New York City, married, and John eventually got a job at Tillinghast coal and lumber in Danielson where he made the deliveries with a horse and wagon. In 1915 Rosie Hatt was born in the red house by the old recycling center road on Packer Road. As she grew older everyone just called her Rose.

Also in this same area, you can see the schoolhouse she attended as a child. When Rose first started school, there were only two windows in the front, but after a few years they added more for better light. At one time there were 35 students because Plainfield sent some children there also.

Ruth Davis was her schoolteacher; she loved the arts and organized several plays that were held in the large meeting room at the Packer Hotel. Rose loved to act, to be involved in plays, pageants, and she loved to memorize and to sing. When she became older, she sang in the Calvary Chapel choir, something she did for more than thirty years.

Packer also had a train depot where Rose would pay a dime to ride to Plainfield to take piano lessons from Mrs. Lyons. However, learning the piano wasn't for her. She would much rather play outdoors. The school had a baseball field where the kids in the neighborhood would play ball and horseshoes. Rose even had a job as a child. She would carry the mail to her neighbors for 5 cents a week.

The hotel was used by people who would visit the Packer Mill. The mill made cotton for several years and then switched to making dyes before it was abandoned.

Her husband, Jim Yaworski, came to visit the area and met Rose and her family when she was a young girl. Jim asked her to begin writing to him and their romance began. They married at a very young age. Six years later Jim, Jr. was born and six years after that Dennis came along. Rose now has nine grandchildren and 17 great grandchildren.

Jim bought a truck and started making deliveries such as grain and fine sand to many chicken farmers who used it as bedding and his trucking business was born. Rose did the books for the business for many years. The first truck that Jim owned (1936 Ford dump truck) is on display at the Yaworski Truck Museum.

Rose loves gardening and has always had a garden. She sold pansies, gladiola and asters to Mckenna, Johnson, Lewis and Holdridge greenhouses. She also had large strawberry beds and sold strawberries. She had a free delivery service: her husband would take the orders to the customers for her.

When asked to name one of the biggest changes in Canterbury, she said having a paved road. Rose remembers that Packer Road would turn into a slippery, impassable mud bog every time it rained. All the neighbors on Packer Road were very grateful when the road was finally paved.

Rose loved the outdoors. The day I visited her she had just mowed the lawn and weeded her garden and tomorrow she planned to do the trimming. Even after all these years she would much rather be outdoors than sit inside.

John Chicos
   --by Steve

John was a forward torpedo man on a submarine in the Pacific in the Second World War. He told about being hunted by the Japanese destroyers which dropped depth charges on them. As the explosions came closer and closer, the level of tension and fear on the sub went up and up, but his sub was never hit.

As John's submarine was observing one island, they spotted a train trestle crossing a bay. Each night a train crossed it, always at the same time. So, the officers came up with a plan to bomb the bridge and destroy the train. They sent out a patrol in a rubber raft to plant explosives on the bridge, then waited for the train to come.

However, that night it did not come at the regular time. Instead a different train came later and as it crossed the bay, they blew up the bridge. It turned out to be a bigger catch then they'd thought, as it was an ammunition train, adding great explosions to the detonation of the bridge. This sub was the only one to ever sink a train.

John T. Bennett
--by Sheila

John T. Bennett's family has been in Canterbury many years, beginning with his maternal grandfather, A. Hale Bennett (born 1860), his mother Dorothy Bradford Bennett (born 1892), his paternal grandfather, Elmer Bennett (born 1863) and his father Arthur C. Bennett (born 1886).

Both of his Grandfathers were veterinarians and his  father, Arthur, was quite an entrepreneur. Arthur was a fur buyer for firms in New York, traveling extensively to buy muskrat, mink, skunk, raccoon and gray and red fox pelts.

He also got into the business of making railroad ties and selling them to the railroad. He had several steam engine sawmills (like the one in the picture above) operating in Canterbury and other locations.

When local filling stations wouldn't give him a discount on gasoline, he decided to open up his own filling station (see picture below) next to his house--the red Colonial house just north of the Canterbury Green. After a time, he also added a soda fountain at the location.

As a boy, John worked at the soda fountain. They had 14  flavors of ice cream, selling their cones for a few cents, but they really made money on the Sundaes because they were 35 cents. They bought milk mainly from Malcolm Wibberley who had a dairy farm on Lisbon Road. John estimates they sold 3,000 gallons of ice cream per year.

The Bennetts first lived on Graff Road, but moved closer to the center of Town on Route 169, as John's mother, Dorothy, was a teacher and taught school at the North Society School. John says before building the Dr. Helen Baldwin School, the graduation ceremonies for each individual school were held at the First Congregational Church on the Green.

Growing up, John spent a lot of time across the street playing with the neighbor children Sally, Lydia, Albert and Oscar Havunen. Along with the Havunens, he attended the Green School with the Davis and Hart children.

Did you know Canterbury had a baseball team? Teams were organized in the 1930's and Canterbury's team played in the vacant lot across from Manship Park. A baseball diamond was maintained there and when the team played others in the area, John Bennett sold candy at the games. He said you could always find the brothers, John and Fred Cone, wearing their baseball team uniforms around town.

John was a member of the 4-H and had took great care of his garden behind the filling station. He is also a lifetime member of the Grange and remembers the good times had by all at the 4th of July clambakes Fred Hicks and Grace Dawley used to put on.

John remembers that in 1929 Route 169 was paved and electricity came to Canterbury. Along with the paving, the Kitt Brook Bridge was constructed. The bridge builders simply put up tents and lived along the side of the road until the bridge was completed, then they paved it and moved on.

In 1930, his Grandfather, A. Hale Bennett, was Judge of Probate and his Father, Arthur, was First Selectman. His Grandfather was unhappy that judges had to retire at 70 years of age according to state statute, so Arthur said "Why don't we switch jobs?", and that's what they did, with Arthur becoming Judge of Probate and Hale becoming First Selectman.

At one time, before World War II, the two successful State Representatives in town and the Judge of Probate agreed to pay for an oyster stew for all Town of Canterbury residents. This was held at the Grange Hall, which was the center of Town activity.

.

146

While at Griswold High School, John would often go hunting with Alfred Utz, but John never paid much attention to Alfred's children, Celia, Fred and Bob, who sometimes tagged along on the trip. Then, in 1942 when he was home from the Army, Alfred drove by in his truck with a pretty young blond girl. "Who's that?" John asked. "Why that's Celia," he was told. "Boy she really grew up!" he said. They were married several years later in 1948.

John was interested in politics, like the rest of the family and he was the Registrar of Voters when voting was changed from paper ballots to voting machines. He was also appointed County Sealer of Weights and Measures. This was a person who inspects gasoline pumps, cotton mill scales, grocery store scales, etc. to make sure they are accurate. After a few years, he became the State inspector.

Canterbury's old records contain so much interesting information and history. It is even a greater pleasure to talk with someone who is a living history book like John T. Bennett.

Kavi Ruuskanen
--by Sheila

The Canterbury Volunteer Fire Department was incorporated in 1947 and had many charter members. In the entire history of the Fire Department, the first non-chartered Canterbury Volunteer Fire Department member to serve for fifty years is  Kalervo (Kavi) Ruuskanen. When Kavi's parents, Otto and Helmi were living in Waterbury, they were looking for a place to start a chicken farm. A woman from Helmi's hometown in Finland, who lived on Kerr Road, told them there was a farm available in Canterbury.

Otto hopped a bus from Waterbury, got off at the Brooklyn Town hall and trudged all the way in the snow to North Canterbury Road (near Wauregan Road) to see the farm and he decided to buy it in March of 1943. He built all the coops--although they are gone now—and the farm house (picture above), which still stands.

Otto had the distinction of being named to the 1928 Olympic cross-country ski team, but unfortunately he was denied the position because he was not a U.S. Citizen. He tried out again in 1952 and came in 11th place.

The family sold eggs commercially as well as to neighbors. When he was a child, Kavi's parents would sort the eggs by size using a single egg scale.

When Kavi started school, he did not speak English so he had to learn it as he went along. Kavi remembers a neighbor, Christian Kerr, taking him, his younger sister, Hilkka (which means Little Red Riding Hood in Finnish), and the neighborhood children to the Congregational church.

He also remembers a neighbor, O. Arnold Kerr and his wife Dorothy Ester Smith Kerr had a vanity license plate using all their initials "OAK DESK". Maybe some of you remember Mrs. Kerr as a teacher at Dr. Helen Baldwin

School. (Comment from Steve) I remember her very well, because, as my second grade teacher, she discovered that I was not able to read. I'd been faking it all along; having an excellent memory, I just repeated what the other students read out loud. She demoted me to the lowest reading group, which was a great incentive to learn to read, and in two weeks I was back in the top group. I am so thankful for her perception and firm direction, making me an avid reader for the rest of my life.

Kavi was very active in 4-H and, after he turned 17, he was involved in a 4-H service club of Windham county which put on the 4-H fair in Woodstock. They did everything from making the flyers, to setting up for events and cleaning the grounds when the fair was over.

Kavi remembers how rural Canterbury used to be when he and his mother would pick blueberries along Route 169 and Wauregan Road.

As a young man Kavi became a member of the Finnish American Heritage Society. When he was a boy, there were weddings, musicals and plays at the Finnish Hall on North Canterbury Road.

He attended Griswold High School, where some of his school mates were David Veit, Julius Vapper, Mary Bingham, Karen Pellinen and Barbara Lindell. Kavi also went to UConn for two years and earned a certificate in poultry farming as he continued to work on the family farm.

In the 1960's if you had a fire, you called the Brooklyn jail. Then the jail would call Lillian Waskiewicz at Ed's Garage and Lillian would call a third of the Town firefighters on her list to come to the fire.

One day Kavi was at Ed's Garage when a call came in and a firefighter, David Veit, asked Kavi to come and help. Back then they had a portable water pump that weighed a couple hundred pounds that had to be dragged to the nearest water source and he helped do that as well as using brooms and rakes to put out the brush fire. After that first experience, he decided to join the Volunteer Fire Department.

In those days, one of the more difficult tasks the Volunteer Fire Department members had to do when a storm came, was to help cut the fallen trees so the power Company could get through and restore power. When hurricane Gloria came through town, it left a lot of work for the Fire Department members.

Kavi was also involved in the Canterbury paper drives for the Fire Department. As a volunteer, he would go house-to-house and collect newspapers and other paper products and bring it back to a big trailer truck to be packed in and hauled away to be sold. He reminded me that he came to my father's farm on North Society Road to pick up paper feed bags.

Kavi was also one of the original six EMT's when the Canterbury ambulance was put into service in 1975/76. The others were David Veit, Glen Veit, Luther Thurlow, Ted Berbrick and Alfred Coderre.

In 1965 Kavi joined the Connecticut State Police as an Auxiliary Trooper. Because he had this training, Alfred Utz asked him to become a Canterbury Constable. He ran for the position in 1971, was elected and has served as a Canterbury Constable for nearly forty years.

Hearing about the many years Kavi has volunteered reminds me of a quote by Marjorie Moore: "Volunteering is the ultimate exercise in democracy. You vote in elections once a year, but when you volunteer, you vote every day about the kind of community you want to live in." Kavi has certainly made Canterbury a better place to live.

Ken Swan 1932
--by Steve

Ken was born in Montville in 1932. In 1948 his father bought a 154 acre farm in Canterbury, located where Ed's Wasko's gravel bank is now on Route 169, next to the cemetery.

Ken joined the Coast Guard in 1952 and served on a buoy tender in New York Harbor before being transferred to the Coast Guard Academy. There he served as an instructor of rope and cable splicing, and also oversaw the task of keeping all the sailboats in good order.

He got out of the service in 1954 and returned to his father's farm to help with the 38 milk cows. His father also had a small gravel business and Ken would make deliveries for him in a little Chevy truck.

Then Ken started working for Cliff Williams driving truck and running Cliff's big shovel. In the picture to the left, Ken stands on the shovel some 60 years later! Below him are Denis Yaworski, Bob West and

seated is Cliff Williams.

In 1959 Ken went into business for himself with his tractor and backhoe doing cellars, septic systems and driveways. He worked up until he was 80 years old. He had seven children, including his step children, and now has five great grandchildren.

Lew Gray

--by Sheila

In 1916 Hendrik and Florine Verkade came to America from Holland. They arrived at Ellis Island and eventually settled in New London, Connecticut. Hendrik had had a nursery in Holland and wanted to start one in Connecticut. In preparation, he would take his wheelbarrow and trim trees in the neighborhood so he could gather seeds and with these eventually started Verkade's nursery.

In the 1940's Lew Gray came home from the service and worked for Hendrik. During winter months, the nursery workers would work in the greenhouse and do plant cuttings. One day Lew was brought into the greenhouse and happened to be seated next to Hendrik's daughter Lillian. Lew was amazed at Lillian's speed, but it was easy for her because she had been doing this job since she was 11 years old. Lew and Lillian hit it off, married and eventually had four children: Patricia, Lew, Michael and Tom.

Hendrik decided to expand his successful nursery business and asked Lew and Lillian if they would start a location in Canterbury. It was a good opportunity and they moved to Canterbury in 1955 when there were only 6 or 7 houses on Brooklyn Road.

Lillian (a city girl) thought she was going to the end of the world, but she was happy to do it for Lew. Lew liked the location because the land was flat and he saw good potential for planting. For a brief time, he even used a horse to till the fields. For many years, the nursery kept a mule for cultivating the narrow strips of land between the rows and Russel Cook was the "mule man," adept at keeping the creature moving while avoiding any kicks that might come his way.

When asking individuals if they knew anyone who worked for Lou they said, "Almost every teenager in Canterbury worked at Verkades Nursery!" I talked to several of his former workers who described their job to me: planting trees, weeding, loading trees into trucks, unloadjng peat moss from Canada and hoeing rows.

152

Steve Wibberley described what it was like working there. "We'd arrive on a sunny Saturday morning, gather in the shed outside the office, waiting for Lew to give us our instructions. Then he'd load us into his venerable Chevy Suburban and drive us to the field we were to weed that day. The rows seemed to stretch on forever, and the sun was often hot, so I looked forward to the noon lunch break. The afternoons were as long as the rows, but it was good to get that paycheck at the end of a Saturday."

Many remember working with supervisors, Ronald St. Onge and Russell Cook. One said Lew would sometimes gather the workers around and say, "Time for a lecture." He would proceed to give them a talk on life lessons, such as "put your money away for a rainy day".

One of the Gray's neighbors was Charles Lawson. He played the violin and harmonica and told the Grays that there used to be square dances held in their original farmhouse before the Gray's moved in. Interestingly enough, Mr. Lawson was the driver for the town doctor, Dr. Helen Baldwin, when she made house calls around town.

One day Lew took his 6-year old daughter, Pat, to school and discovered there was just a flimsy Venetian blind between the grades located in the gymnasium/lunch room, and it was difficult for the children to hear the teacher. Seeing this need started Lew's interest in serving the community.

Lew joined the Republican Party and became part of the campaign to vote for construction of a better school building to provide all the children with a better learning situation.

Lew and Lillian's daughter, Pat, wanted to join 4-H, so Lillian became a leader for her daughter's group. When the boys wanted to join 4-H, there weren't any groups in this area, so Lew started a 4-H group and over time about 25-30 boys joined it. He formed a farm and garden club and they would met at the Gray's barn to do projects such as making wreaths at Christmas time.

Many years later, Ken Beauchene sent Lillian a letter telling her how much that 4-H group meant to him when he was a boy. It made such an impression on him that all of his children joined a 4-H group near where they lived.

The original Canterbury Firehouse was where Creative Interiors is today. Lew became a member of the Canterbury Fire Department remained on as a life member.

He always helped with the Fire Department barbeques and horse shows. In the 1960's the Fire Department sponsored a yearly horse show that was held where Ed's Garage gravel bank is today. Approximately 800 to 900 horses entered every year and the event was held over a ten-year period.

Lew was also involved in building the new firehouse on Route 14 and was on the committee to acquire Canterbury's first ambulance.

Lew was elected as First Selectman from 1971 to 1977. One thing still true today in the First Selectman's office is that he would get calls about water running over the roads because the beavers dammed a pond. He enlisted the help of Alton Olomoski to trap and get rid of the beavers.

Does anyone remember Lew participating in the dunking booth on 4th of July? He had an outgoing personality and I remember him teasing the crowd and daring them to dunk him.

He was often heard to say he could not have done the First Selectman's job without Marguerite Simpson (Town Clerk 1966 – 1985). Many years later, Lew served the Town again on the Board of Finance 1997 to 2005.

Lew assisted the Recreation Commission when they created Manship Park. He was glad to get involved because when his children were young, they were all into sports and he believed in making a place where children could play and enjoy being outdoors.

He was the Vice President of the Cemetery Association Board of Directors and was a sexton. He was a Lions Club charter member and a member of the VFW. Lew served in World War II and even after he got married he was called back to serve in the Korean War.

As a nurseryman, Lew was President of the Connecticut Nurseryman's Association, and the Eastern Region Nurseryman's Association, as well as being a member of the International Plant Propagators Society, the New England Nurseryman's Association; and, as a prominent businessman, he was on the Board of Directors for the Brooklyn Savings Bank.

Lew also had a pulley collection that started when a  friend gave him three different pulleys. Lew and the collection were featured in the January 1986 Yankee Magazine (see picture to left). According to the article, half of his 2,000 pulleys were displayed on the walls of his basement.

Lew worked very hard at everything he did and he had the natural ability to be a great leader. He loved Canterbury and loved devoting his time to help not only children, but everyone. One former worker said Lew Gray is fondly remembered as a good neighbor, a good friend and a good man to work for.

Linwood Tracy 1911-2013
--by Sheila and Steve

Can you imagine holding the same political office for sixty-three years? We had such a man in Canterbury who has been a Justice of the Peace since 1938 and his name is Linwood Tracy.

The first time I met Mr. Tracy, he was a teacher at Calvary Chapel's Vacation Bible School. He was outgoing, had a big booming voice and a hearty laugh. Having a shy nature, I was a little bit afraid of him, but it turned out that there was nothing to be afraid of, as Linwood encouraged all of his students to be themselves.

The Tracy family has been in Canterbury since it was founded in 1703. In the 1800's his Grandfather, Lucius, operated Canterbury's pauper farm, where poor people could live and work. This farmhouse is the one-story building located across the street from the post office. Some of the residents were the Quinebaug Indians.

Linwood has lived in Canterbury his whole life. except for two or three years when the family moved to Woodstock where his father, Herbert, ran that town's pauper farm.

Linwood's childhood was not a happy one. His mother died when he was about six years old when they lived in Woodstock. After moving back to Canterbury, his father remarried and his step mother brought two sons of her own

into the marriage, which set up difficult dynamics. Linwood attended the Green School and in the picture below he is on the left end of the middle row in a black shirt. He does not look happy.

When Linwood was in the 4th or 5th grade, his father, Herbert, bought a team of horses and worked for Arthur Bennett who

156

operated a sawmill and filling station.

At that time, Linwood had a trap line where he caught skunks and muskrats. He checked it each morning before going to school and would sell the pelts he got to Mr. Bennett for some spending money. The skins were probably dyed and used as hand muffs, which were popular at the time.

The Tracy family didn't have a lot to eat, so Linwood supplemented the table by hunting. One time when he was after deer, a Blue Jay followed him squawking warnings and scaring off any game. After a while Linwood had had enough and shot the bird. Just then a game warden came along and fined him for killing a song bird. Linwood said from that time on he had little liking for game wardens!

Hanging May baskets on the door of one's favorite girl or boy, then knocking on the door, and hiding was a common practice. The child in the house would then come out and try and find the gift giver. Linwood had a crush on Truman Hart's daughter, Helen, and she was the recipient of his May basket.

Being a farm town, many families in Canterbury belonged to the Grange, as the Tracy family did, too, and one of their favorite activities was singing. Linwood's father formed a quartet and Linwood and Anna Herr would sing duets.

Linwood passed on his love of music to all around him and had all four of his children play an instrument or sing. Linwood also brought his love of music to Calvary Chapel where he led singing, while his wife and daughters played piano and organ. That love of music has stayed, as now a fourth generation of musicians, trained by Linwood's daughter, Clair Ellston, carry on his positive influence.

At age thirteen, Linwood graduated from the Green school but couldn't get working papers so he had to go back to Frost school (on Lisbon Road) for one more year.

As a boy, Linwood had several hobbies. In the winter you could always find him skating, in the fall he would hunt and trap. In the spring, he and a buddy would sometimes come down "sick" and be sent home from school, but would make a miraculous recovery on the way home and be able to go fishing.

Fourth of July celebrations were a big event in Canterbury when Linwood was a boy. Linwood's father ran the clambake at the Grange hall where there were fireworks and lots of activities. Linwood and several other boys would sneak into the church on the Green and ring the bell at midnight on July 4th. This went on for about three years until they were caught by Merritt Hawes and were "persuaded" to stop.

In the picture right, Linwood is on the right, then his siblings Ida, Morris, Edith, and little Walter. As children, Linwood and his two sisters and two brothers didn't have any transportation and the only way to  get around, was to walk, so they walked everywhere and thought nothing of it.

Linwood remembers the first paved road in Canterbury, about 1922 which came from Brooklyn and was paved up to the intersection of Route 169 and Route 14. Then it turned on Route 14 toward Scotland until it reached what is now Creative Interiors. It was 1928 or 29 before the road was paved from the Routes 169/14 intersection to Lisbon.

In his teen years Linwood formed a gang of friends, who called themselves the "Rinky Dinks." One of their games was auto tag, where one of them would park in the bushes, waiting for another to come along and then would zoom out and "tap" the other car. Cars in those days were a lot more rugged than what we have today, as they could take a "tap" and not be totaled!.

His teen years were particularly unhappy, so with the help of the Rinky Dinks, Linwood built a cabin on Buck Hill Road and lived there on his own. That cabin still stands and is lived in, having been added onto several times.

He got a job working at a laundry service in Plainfield

where his boss wanted him to make deliveries and for this he needed a driver's license. So, he drove his employer's truck to the MVD, took his test and got his license. The inspector never asked how he got there!

In his twenties Linwood and his friends were into drinking, often making their own liquor in a bathtub. One of his friends went blind from drinking a bad batch.

On the land where St. Augustine's Church is located today, there was formally a hoop shop. This was a place that made oak hoops for ship masts and yardarms. The oak was steamed and bent into shape and tacked with copper nails. Linwood's grandfather worked for the shop owner, who was the grandfather of the woman who later became his wife, Althea Williams. (in the picture at right with Linwood)

At first Linwood was interested in Althea's sister, but he discovered that Althea was more of a fun person and she was the one he decided to marry.

His proposal statement was, "If you don't marry me, I'm going to join the navy." Althea accepted his proposal and in August of 1933, they eloped and got married, keeping it a secret for four months--except from Linwood's employer, a farmer who gave him a room to sleep in. This actually came out without their planning it. One morning when the farmer's wife went in to make Linwood's bed, there was a girl in it! Below are pictures of Linwood and Althea about the time of their marriage

Althea was a kind and gentle person, but she had a very strong constitution and would not be moved from what she believed.

They didn't have much to eat after they were married, so Althea would go out and shoot something for supper--a raccoon, opossum, rabbit, or whatever crossed her path. One time when they were both out hunting, Althea said something to Linwood, which he didn't understand, but then she shot and a raccoon fell out a tree right on top of him! They laughed a lot about that and told the story often to others.

One time Linwood and a friend went hunting and got a deer. They loaded in into the trunk of his car and took it home. Linwood backed the car up to the house and opened the cellar doors. Then when he opened the trunk, the deer, which was not as dead as they thought, jumped out and ran into the cellar. They followed it, wrestled it to the floor and dispatched it with a pocket knife.

After they married, Linwood continued his wild living with drinking, racing around in his car and poaching. Then in 1935 he and Althea went to a meeting in the Nazarene church in Danielson with Jim & Rose Yaworski.

Linwood said it was like the speaker knew everything Linwood had ever done and he came under great conviction for his sinful living. At the end of the service he went forward and accepted Christ as his Savior, as did Althea, Jim and Rose. It was a new and dramatic beginning for them all.

They all started going to Calvary Chapel. Linwood and Althea also started a Bible study, along with Jim and Rose, and then began to go to churches to sing and preach.

 Linwood worked most of his life at Electric Boat as a machinist, and openly shared his faith with the other workers. Early on he led a coworker to accept Christ as his Lord and Savior. Then the man asked Linwood why he was still smoking as a Christian. Linwood quit right on the spot, convicted of his inconsistency, and he never smoked again.

Another of his fellow workers was a heavy drinker and had no interest in the gospel, but Linwood took the man's teenage son to Canterbury for the summer, giving him a break from the chaos in his own home.

In 1938 a group of young Canterbury residents, comprised of Rudy Nikkonen, Nelson Carpenter, Lillian Frink and a few others, formed the young Republicans Club and they each decided what office they would run for. Linwood choose Justice of the Peace and won.

He is very pleased that most of the couples he has married over the years have stayed together. Another part of his job was to be a judge over family matters, traffic violations, fish and game violations, and other minor infractions. The courthouse was in the building next door to the Frink & Wright store and was in operation until 1959.

One case that came before him was a man arrested for shooting a deer out of season. The minimum fine was $100.00, so Linwood fined the man $100.00 and then returned $95.00. The game warden who arrested the man was very upset at this decision, but Linwood felt that since the man had seven children, he should be able to hunt venison to feed his family no matter what time of year it was.

His daughter, Clair, said that people often showed up unannounced at Linwood's house and wanted to get married. So, Linwood's family would quickly rearrange the living room and hold the ceremony, with Althea being the witness.

In this picture below, Linwood sits with three of his four children, left to right Bruce, Clair Ellston and Allyn Woods.

Linwood was also a coin collector. This started when he was attending the Green school and decided to pick some violets along the side of the road for his teacher, Cornelia Lovell. While doing this he found a two-cent coin (which he still has today) and from that time on coins have fascinated him.

His daughter, Clair, described Linwood as a very generous man who loved fun. Several times a year he would pile his kids, the neighbor kids and others into his big old Hudson and take them to Savin Amusement Park in New Haven. He paid for everyone's entrance, rides and food. And he had a wonderful time himself.

One time when a family ran out of gas in front of his house, he went to Ed's garage, bought them 5 gallons of gas, and refused to take anything for it.

He helped others with construction right up into his 90s, as seen in this picture.

All through their married life, Linwood and Althea supplemented their diet and income in any way they could. Linwood would make maple syrup and Althea kept cows, usually three, which she and Linwood milked, and made butter. During the WW II Linwood took butter and maple syrup to EB and sold them to his coworkers, who were happy to have some luxuries during the time of rationing.

They also had chickens and pigs, along with goats for milk, which they sold. With all these animals, they had to cut hay each summer and the whole family pitched in to gather it loose, forking it into the barn. He also got horses for his daughters because he wanted them to have a good childhood. In the snapshot below, Linwood holds his youngest son, Bruce on Clair's horse.

Linwood always had a garden, a big one, and not just to supply the table with food. He loved his gardening, and continued with it all through his life. His children, of course, were drafted to help with the weeding. To encourage them, Linwood would put a case of soda at the end of the long rows.

Linwood also loved fishing and clamming and would take his family out at least once a week in the summer. He himself fished with Althea as long as he could, you can see in the picture above. And he loved eating lobster, as in the picture below

As mentioned, Linwood's faith was very important to him, central to his life. He was very active in Calvary Chapel and I (Steve) remember having him as a Sunday School teacher in fifth and sixth grades. He wanted his students to memorize passages of the Bible and offered 50 cents for every verse they learned by heart.

He also took us students on trips and taught us how to harvest clams and eat them raw, how to shoot a shot gun and how to ride a horse. He was an all-around man who knew how to do many

things. He was a mentor all through my life. I (Steve) visited him when Linwood was about 100 (celebrating his 100th birthday in the picture above), and asked how he was; Linwood answered, "I just can't understand why God could love me so; I'm such a sinner!" He still had the wonder of his salvation and being more in the presence of God every day, he was more aware than ever of how much God has saved him from!

Linwood still had that big booming voice and hearty laugh right to the end, especially when talking about his childhood. I (Sheila) am not afraid of him anymore; instead, I have great respect for him and think of Linwood as a pioneer, of sorts, strong, hardworking, no-nonsense and ingenious.

And I (Steve) credit Linwood with the development of my own faith. As a teenager, typically I was critical of what went on in the lives of people in the church. But I had to admit that Linwood consistently lived what he said he believed, an example of true faith. And that kept me searching until I came to my own surrender to Christ at age 23. And then Linwood acted as my mentor for many more years.

He drove until he was 95; he only turned in his license because, he said, "If I have an accident, even if it's the other driver's fault, they'll say it was my fault because I'm 95!" And he gardened until he was almost 100. Below after harvesting one of his giant squashes, he sits with his son Bruce

Linwood had a good, strong constitution and lived to be 102 and 8 months old, well cared for by his daughter, Allyn and her husband, Don Woods.

Lloyd Anderson 1942
--by Steve

Lloyd "Andy" Anderson was born in Valparaiso, Indiana in 1942. He went to Valparaiso University for three semesters, and then joined the Navy in 1962. The Vietnam war was on, so instead of getting drafted, he decided to get into the submarine service.

He said his recruiter promised him an assignment in submarine work, but Lloyd realized later that such a promise was empty, for he had to pass several tests to qualify. He did, however, pass them and ended up being stationed at the Sub Base in New London.

His Chief was from Voluntown and invited a crew member to go with him to Beach Pond. This crew member later took Andy there, where he met Catheryn Hanson, a Canterbury girl who was teaching at Griswold High. She invited Andy to go swimming with her, and their relationship was off and running. It was mostly long distance, as Andy shortly left for three months of submarine duty. They got engaged on Christmas eve, 1965 and were going to wait until

Andy got out of the Navy in 1969.

However, following his tour of duty in Scotland, Andy got orders to go to Idaho where he would have no sea duty. So, they decided to marry earlier, in 1966. That meant Catheryn had only three months to put together a wedding, but she did it well and Andy got there in time with Bob Manship as his best man, making a successful start on their marriage.

Catheryn finished out her year of teaching in Griswold and joined Andy in Idaho where she was able to find a teaching job. They stayed there for 2 years.

In the Fall of 1968 I (Steve) was on my motorcycle trip to Alaska, and somehow got in touch with Andy, asking if

165

I could stop by their rented condo while passing through Idaho. They said fine, however they would not be there when I came, and would leave a key with the neighbor.

So when I pulled up to their condo on my motorcycle, with my leathers, long hair and beard, the neighbor surprisingly unhesitatingly handed over the key.

It had been several days since I'd been able to shower, so I was very thankful for Andy and Catheryn's hospitality, taking several showers before leaving the next day.

When Andy got out of the Navy, they moved back East, finding an apartment in Lisbon. He was hoping to become a state trooper, but that didn't work out. He then got involved in union politics, and decided to become a union lawyer. He went back to school, doing three years of undergrad at UConn, graduating in 1974, and then three more in law school, graduating in 1977.

By the time he became a lawyer, the job with the union was no longer available, so Andy found a place at the law firm of Fred Hulth in New London. Andy's experience in inland wetlands was what got him in.

Meanwhile, Andy Schrader, the lawyer in Canterbury, decided to close his practice and become a dairy farmer in upstate New York. Lloyd decided to fill this legal vacuum and opened an office in Canterbury while still working part time in New London.

After Catheryn's father, Hans, died, they moved to Canterbury in September of 1982 so they could live with and

take care of Catheryn's mother, Lucy. They put an addition on the house and an addition onto their family, as their son, Kent, was born in December of 1982.

Andy and Catheryn both had a liking for foreign sports cars. In the picture here, Andy and Catheryn are enjoying his 1954 MG TD. They later purchased a Porsche, which was the envy of Catheryn's male high school students.

166

In the picture to the left are Andy, Catheryn and Kent enjoying a day at the beach as a family.

As Andy got settled into life in Canterbury and began practicing law there, Marilyn Burris asked him to become part of the Republican town committee, now that he was a resident. He joined the committee and served for many years, becoming chairman at one point.

Andy ran for first selectman twice, but did not make it. He was later elected to the to board of finance, where he served with Lew Grey. Andy continued on the board for a good number of years, several of them as the chairman.

In 1995 Catheryn, who was teaching again at Griswold, had a fall on Easter weekend and collapsed the next day, dying before she arrived at the hospital. It turned out, she had undiagnosed adult onset leukemia, resulting in an enlarged spleen which ruptured when she fell. It was a very sad and sudden turn of events in Lloyd and Kent's lives.

After three years of being single, in 1998 Lloyd married a widow, Joyce, the daughter of Art and Helen LeBeau. They lived in Lloyd's house with Lucy Hanson, caring for her until her death.

Andy continued with his good lawyering until he and Joyce left for Georgia in September of 2016. So, no more seeing Andy driving around town, wearing his sun hat in his little Chrysler convertible with the top down, from March to October.

I can vouch for Andy being a good and reasonable lawyer. He had a sign in the office building pointing to his office that said, "Honest lawyer one flight up," and that was true.

In 1998, when I was going to build my little house on the edge of Echoland Farm on Lisbon Road, the bank directed me to a lawyer in Norwich to do the title search. He wanted $750, although he had just done a search on the same title three months earlier for another transaction. I tried to bargain with him, but to no avail. So, I disregarded the bank's advice and went to Andy. He did the job for $200! Much more reasonable.

When my siblings and I were trying to work out an estate plan for my parents, one of my brothers had us go to a high powered and high priced specialist, who after spending an hour and a half with us (at $500 an hour), declined to give us any advice. "Here are the facts, make your own decision," she said.

So, I went to Andy and he gave us good, down to earth, clear guidelines that worked out very well in the end. He said he was just a country lawyer, but he had more insight than those who presented themselves as experts!

He was also generous. I can't count the number of

 times I called or visited Andy for some legal advice, and when I asked him what my bill was, he would say either, "Don't worry about it," or "I'll send you one," but never did.

When he and Joyce married, she came with grandchildren, which Lloyd seemed to enjoy. Here is Lloyd holding one under Joyce's supervision.

I, for one, was sorry to see him and Joyce leave town, but with some grandchildren in the South where winters are easy and old age is cushioned, you have to go!

Lucy Baldwin 1870-1950 (approximately)
--by Sheila and Pricilla Botti

Miss Lucy, as she was widely known in Canterbury, was Dr. Helen Baldwin's sister. In the following article by Priscilla Smith Botti, posted by Sheila Mason Gayle, we get some insight into Miss Lucy's rich and giving character.

God Turned the Wheels

Dolly, the kind and patient bay horse, stood at the hitching post. The old two-seated wagon held several children impatiently waiting for Miss Lucy. "Will we need umbrellas today?" we called, watching her hold a handkerchief over her head as she hastened toward us. "No," she answered. "The wind is in the west. We'll have a beautiful day." Unhitching the horse, she climbed nimbly into the wagon. With an affectionate command to Dolly, the weekly, and always wonderful, going-to-church expedition started. Church was four miles away. Sometimes the trip was wet and cold,

sometimes hot and dusty. But it was never tiresome.

Miss Lucy was fifty-five years old and I was six when I started going to church with her, but she looked much older. Her ideas were old-fashioned and so were her clothes, (as she appears here standing before the Baldwin house on Route 169) but her heart was young and she made the Primary Department an exciting adventure. Hers was a heart at peace with God and her fellowmen. That was the secret of her greatness. It drew us to her, and brought her influence into our lives to stay.

169

As we rode together to church, she taught us to recognize the beauty in everything around us. When she reined Dolly into the brook for her morning drink, she made sure we noticed the clean washed stones, the seasonal changes of the trees and ferns, the flowers from first buds to last blooms.

As we wound along the dirt road, she taught us the books of the Bible, the twelve sons of Jacob, the Ten Commandments, the Beatitudes. We sang hymns to varied accompaniment. Sometimes it was the sweet notes of spring peep-frogs, the drone of a summer locust, the rustle of fall leaves, or. the crunch of early snow. Each served in turn, but always there was the melody of the turning of the wheels.

In the wooded section, black birch grew by the roadside. Miss Lucy would reach out and break off a branch and give each of us a small piece. How we loved to nibble the bark!

She picked up so many passengers enroute that the bigger boys and girls took turns running on ahead and then riding. As we rounded the last bend, the church bells were always ringing. "Come, come, come," was the message Miss Lucy said they were ringing. "Go, go, go," the boys laughingly echoed, but Miss Lucy only smiled.

Coming home, she tossed out Sunday-school papers to every house. If there were any sick people or shut-ins, she sent one of us to the door with church flowers.

Once a year we went at night, and that was the grandest experience of all. On Christmas Eve we had a big tree in church. We spoke pieces, sang songs and received presents. But even the presents were nothing compared with that exciting Christmas ride.

Lanterns hung from each side of the wagon. Our feet wandered from warm soapstones to mysterious packages. There were last-minute rehearsals for some of us, carols from all of us. Overhead, Miss Lucy pointed out the North Star, the Great Dipper, the Milky Way. As we passed each house she led us in calling out, "Merry Christmas!"

For many years, Miss Lucy took us to church every Sunday, ruts, mud or ice often made traveling difficult and hazardous-but we always got through. Nothing seemed too much for the bay horse and the old lady. Each depended on the other, and neither ever let the other down. I took it for granted then, but looking back; I realize there were more than the two of them. Dolly pulled the wagon, Miss Lucy held the reins, but surely God turned the wheels.

Luther Thurlow 1946
   --by Steve

Luther was born in 1946 in Sturbridge Mass, one of fourteen

children. In this picture are eleven of them with their father, around 1959.

Luther contracted Polio when he was nine and consequently missed a year of school. His family moved to Canterbury in August of 1960, just in time to start school. They settled into a big house on Elmdale Road, just below the junction with Bennet Pond Road. His father worked at the Kaman Plant in Moosup as an inspector of helicopter blades.

Shortly after moving to Canterbury Mrs. Thurlow had her fourteenth child, Phillip. Mr. Thurlow went to the school and got his oldest daughter, Dolly, so she could look after the younger children at home while he took his wife to the hospital.

Luther said that after his mother got home from the hospital, my (Steve's) mother, Virginia, dropped in and offered to do some laundry for Mrs. Thurlow. With fourteen children, there was certainly plenty to be done! In this picture is his mother with six of her children.

Luther got a job mowing the neighbor's lawn. One day he ran out of gas in the middle of the job, and while refilling the tank, the lawn mower caught on fire. No real damage done, but the fire chief, Merritt Hawes came down and gave Luther a lecture on fire safety.

Luther wasn't much for school and left in the 10th

grade. For his first job, he joined his oldest brother, Harry, working for Max Wibberley in his tire shop, where one of his duties was milking the one Guernsey cow Max still had. This was a harbinger of how Luther would spend a lot of his working life.

From the tire shop he moved to working on Gus Campbell's farm on Route 169 for 90 cents an hour. Along with farming, Gus plowed snow for the town and one of Luther's jobs was to ride in the back of the truck in the snowstorm and shovel sand into the sander, a cold and dangerous work.

At age 18 he married Lorraine Miller and got a job at UConn milking cows in the university farm, a job he held for the next 20 years. Luther may not have liked school, but he had no aversion to learning, going on to get his high school diploma and then to become a real estate agent.

He was trying to sell his house on Colburn Road when Carl Boecher came along and offered to give Luther a part time job in his real estate firm. Luther continued his job at UConn while selling real estate on the side. He later worked for Gene Blumenthal, and eventually got his own license in 1981

When the Usetalla family wanted to sell their farm holdings, Luther took that on. Forty-three of the acres were across the street from Calvary Chapel and were being rented by the Burroughs brothers to plant corn.

Since the town was talking about building another school, Luther spoke with First Selectman, David Ginnetti, about how appropriate spot was for it.

They found that the State would pay for 68% of the cost of the land, meaning the town would only have to pay $30,000 for the forty-three acres. The problem was, there was no money for it in the budget, so the town would have to vote on it.

The State did a thorough investigation of the land and presented the very positive findings at a town meeting; they wanted a vote by the fifty or so citizens who were there to see what the interest was. Following the presentation, one of the selectman said, "Well, I'd like to have a Cadillac, but can only

afford a Chevy. I don't think the town can afford this." This seemed to sway the crowd and the proposal was voted down. Several years later the town paid three times that amount for just a parcel of that land to build the present town hall and library.

After hearing the presentation, Luther realized what a perfect piece of land this was for commercial use, with 2,000 feet of frontage, lots of gravel, and a central location. So, he began visiting the businessmen in town, looking for partners who would put up part of the money to buy and develop the land.

In the end, he found seven. One of the partners had a connection with UConn and got students to come and survey the town to see what was needed and wanted in town. The number one desire was for a pharmacy and number two was for a convenience store.

Luther and his partners began the project that has produced the Post Office, the Town Hall, the mall with the Savings Institute, Dinos and several smaller businesses, along with Cumberland Farms and its convenience store,

On another front, Chuck, Luther's brother, was very involved in the Boy Scouts. He wanted to take his troop of 12 boys on a five-mile hike and arranged with Luther for them to camp out at Luther's new home on Colburn road, next to the pond he'd just had dug.

The boys set up camp, built a fire to cook supper, and got ready for bed. Just then a big thunder storm came in. Chuck ran over and asked Luther if they could move their camp into Luther's walk-in basement, which he agreed to.

But shortly after getting settled there, lighten struck the power lines and was transmitted to the grounds in cellar. Blue lightening was bouncing off the walls, which sent the boys scampering upstairs. Luther then agreed to have them camp in the living room for the night. It was a very successful camping

174

trip: nobody died and they all kept dry.

With his brother Chuck, Luther started Windham Real Estate and Investment, selling modular homes. They sold 141 houses in the first two years, all over New England.

Chuck developed an interesting way of advertising their product. On the day a sold house was to be set on the foundation by a crane, Chuck invited all the neighbors to watch, setting up tables for free refreshments. Luther said they almost always sold another home from the contacts they made on that day.

Luther was active in many areas of public life. He was Fire chief in Canterbury for four years in the early 70s. Luther was also the Republican Town Chair for several years in the late 80s and early 90s. He has served on the Canterbury Board of Health for the last twenty years. He has also been the Emergency Management Director (originally called the civil defense coordinator) since 1978 and would like to hand the job over to someone younger. He said that since 2005 it's gotten much more technical and complicated.

He worked to set up a shelter in town in case of an emergency that would make it necessary for people to leave their homes. The Middle School was designated as the shelter and Luther got a generator for the school, an almost new one from the convalescent home in Windham center when they built a new building. He also got one for town hall.

In response to some bureaucratic problems in town, Dave Ginnetti and Luther started a business men's association in Canterbury that had 104 members at one time. It only lasted a couple of years, but served its purpose

On the next page is a picture of Luther withseven of his brothers. All but one of these owned their own business and were productive men involved in their communities.

Back row: Andrew, Luther, Carl, Chuck,
Phillip. Front row, Keith, Tommy, and Mark.

Lydia Greenstein 1920-2011
-by Sheila

In the 1920's the Erickson family--Eric, Lyti and baby Lydia--
traveled around Canterbury in their wagon pulled by Harry,
the horse. It was the family's only transportation and Harry
brought the family wherever they needed to go.

In 1920, when Lydia was only ten weeks old, the
Ericksons moved to Canterbury from New York City to a
house across the street from Lyti's sister, Emma Eastlund,
whose family owned the local grist mill on Tracy Road.

Lydia was an only child, but there were lots of children
nearby to play with-- her cousins Emma, Lucy, Charlie, Ina
and Helen Eastlund, and Helen and Anna Romanoff, as well
as Kenneth, Glen, Karl, Marilyn and David Veit. In the winter
they would all go sledding right down the middle of the Tracy
Road since there was no traffic. Lydia learned how to swim
and skate on the Eastlund pond across the street.

One of her family's traditions was the steam bath on
Saturday nights followed by coffee and cake. Time was also
spent at the Finnish Hall where lots of dancing and music
filled the night.

Lydia loved music. She started violin lessons at five
years old with a Mr. Pope and took piano lessons from Mrs.
Hawes. As an adult, she studied voice in New York and I will
always remember her beautiful sacred music solos during
Sunday morning church services.

Lydia also liked to read and so she would go the
Library in the original Town Hall, located in the spot where
the Calvary Chapel parsonage is today. The Librarian was
Mable Kinne and only allowed three books to be taken out at
one time, so Lydia would take them out on Friday and read all
three by the end of the weekend.

Most of all, Lydia loved Jesus. Her faith was important
to her and she sought to live it out every day. Her daughter,
Liisa, provided me with a copy of the prayer that Lydia had
written out as an adult to begin her relationship with God:
"Thank you, God, for loving me and for sending your Son to
die for my sins. I sincerely repent of my sins and receive Jesus

Christ as my personal Savor. Now, as your child, I turn my entire life over to you. Amen."

Did you know Canterbury once had a maternity hospital? It was located near the intersection of Route 14 and Lisbon Road. Lydia remembers that a registered nurse, Nina Hansen (Fred Sacket's sister), was in charge. Her friend, Dorothy Green, was born there.

When Lydia went to High School she had to walk from her house out to Route 14 to get the school bus. She was in the first graduating class of Griswold High School in 1937.

She met her husband, Ted Greenstein, at her cousin, Helen Eastlund Nyland's wedding. Together they raised their three children Liisa, Eric, Carol along with a foster daughter, Chris.

Lydia was involved in many activities such as PTA, 4-H and director of Calvary Chapel junior choir. Eventually, she became involved in politics starting out as a Selectmen's Clerk to Bob Laws and then was elected as Canterbury's Town Clerk in 1963. The Treasurer's job was later added to the Town Clerk position as well. When she retired from the position, she suggested that Margurite Simpson run and Mrs. Simpson won.

Lydia enjoyed travel and went to Alaska, Hawaii, the Caribbean, Europe and the Panama Canal to name a few vacation destinations.

One of the best times she had traveling was with her grandchildren. She took them to all the places of their heritage in Finland, Norway, Russia and Poland so they could know where they were from. As a matter of fact, she celebrated her 80th birthday in Iceland.

She lived in Florida for a time and then moved back to Canterbury. She said when you come back home and talk to the people you knew as a child, they are the same and it was like you were never away, but you also remember places that were once cornfields and now they are developed. Lydia said she enjoyed life and she enjoyed herself wherever she was.

Below in the picture on left is Lydia as young woman with spunk; in middle are Ted and Lydia, on the right Lydia later in life.

Marguerite Simpson 1919-2009

--by Sheila

Marguerite Simpson was a modern woman with a forceful personality, direct communication and was well ahead of her time. She was a wife and mother, held political office involving multiple positions, was a fabulous cook and seamstress, musician and advocate. She has done it all while living in Canterbury.

There are still a few Canterbury citizens who were born in Canterbury and remain here. Marguerite Tracy was born on Depot Road in 1919. The house she was born in is still standing at the sharp corner of Depot Road just North of Shagbark Lane.

Anyone who went to school in Canterbury in the 30's, 40's and 50's will remember her mother, Happie K. Tracy, who was a teacher and also was the Post Mistress when Marguerite was born.

At that time, Canterbury had a train depot/Post office there in South Canterbury, as it was called. The mail and passenger train would travel from Providence to Hartford and stop in Canterbury twice a day.

Marguerite's father, Arthur, would take the train to work at the Plainfield <u>Laughton</u> Mill until he got a car. The train depot was eventually brought by Mr. Underhill's father-in-law and moved to South Canterbury Road; P.B. Smith later bought it and turned it into his residence.

When the mail drop was changed to the center of Canterbury, Happie gave up the Post Mistress job, went into teaching and the family moved to Lisbon Road where Marguerite attended Frost School. Eventually the family settled on Tracy Road.

Marguerite's family was very musical. Her Aunt Ida would play piano for Marguerite's father Arthur and her Uncle Burt when they sang at the socials held at the Canterbury Grange Hall. Many dances were held at the Grange and that made Marguerite very happy since dancing was her favorite hobby. The Finnish Hall was also very active and she would go to their dances as well. Mr. Usetello would drive anybody interested going to the hall and he was also the entertainment as he played the accordion.

In the thirties, many students could not go on to high school because they had to get a job. However, because education was highly valued in the Tracy family, Marguerite was encouraged to attend Plainfield High School. This is where she learned to sew and became an excellent seamstress. She graduated in 1937 and then continued her education by attending Morse School of Business.

She took piano lessons in Canterbury from Elsie Hawes and later in Willimantic, along with her friend, Margaret Robinson. She played the piano for Calvary Chapel and was a Sunday school teacher for many years.

When she met her husband, Charlie Simpson, he lived i n the Packerville section of Canterbury. Charlie's sister Georgeanna (Wellinghausen) decided Charlie needed somebody and thought he and Marguerite would make a good match. She was right, they were married for 55 years before his death and had five children.

Marguerite and Charlie put great importance on their faith and were life-long members at Calvary Chapel. Charlie make a commitment to Christ while he was in the army, and Marguerite came to faith during days after Calvary Chapel come into existence.

Marguerite served in many capacities in the church, one of them being a Sunday School teacher. She was my (Steve) teacher and mentor all through high school and I would often visit her later on to talk over issues and to listen to her wisdom. She was at times rough and blunt, but she always spoke truth and we knew she loved us.

Marguerite followed her father, who was an Assessor, into politics. She and her brother Darwin both took an interest in his work. During this time, the First Selectmen, Norman Kerr, asked Marguerite to help him with some paperwork for the Selectmen's Office. She eventually joined the Republican Town Committee and became Town Treasurer.

Before the addition was added to the Dr. Helen Baldwin School in 1962, all the Town records were kept in elected officials' homes and if you needed to get some town business done you went directly to the home of the Town

Clerk, Tax Collector or Assessor.

Jeanette White was the first Town Clerk to move the town offices into the basement of the Dr. Helen Baldwin School.

Lydia Greenstein was the next Town Clerk, but when she decided she didn't want to run again, Priscilla Botti said to Marguerite, who was still the town Treasurer at the time, "You need to run!" She did and won the election in 1966 and remained the Canterbury Town Clerk and treasurer until 1973 when she resigned as Treasurer, but was appointed as the Town Clerk/Tax Collector. She held these two positions until 1985.

She remembers when Bob Manship became First Selectmen. It was Bob's first time in politics and not realizing that the Town Clerk is independent, he thought it was his job to tell Marguerite how to do her job. If you know Marguerite, she clearly spoke her mind and Bob realized he was not in charge of the Town Clerk's office! After that discussion, he and Marguerite had a great relationship.

Her value of education carried over into her job as Town clerk. She attended classes to become certified and was very well read, keeping impeccable records. She made sure Canterbury was in compliance with all the state statutes, even though Canterbury was a small town when Marguerite started her political career. As the town grew, she made sure Canterbury kept up with modern times.

Marguerite and Charlie had five children, Mark, Paul, Judy, Tim and Steve. Marguarite and Charlie's fourth child, Tim was born with Downs Syndrome. At that time there wasn't much support for families with special needs children, but Margartie played a role in changing that. She prodded the State to provide help and services, not just for her son, but for all families with special needs children.

Unlike many Downs Syndrome children, Tim grew up to be quite functional because he was "mainstreamed" in both family and church life. He could sing all the hymns, was a greeter and usher, and was an accepted and loved part of the church family. He went on to be able to live in a group home and provide some for himself in a workshop setting.

Marguerite made all this happen with her vision and persistence.

In the picture on left, are four generations of her family: Marguerite, with her mother, Happie K. Tracy, her daughter-in-law Karen, and her first grandson.

Near the end of her life, Marguerite moved to Oregon where her daughter cared for her until the end, the end of a long, positive and influential life.

Below on left are Marguerite and Charlie, and on the right, Marguerite at work in the town office.

Bulletin photo by Randy Flaum
Marguerite Simpson will be retiring as Canterbury's Town Clerk.

Here is Marguerite's family in the late 60s. Back row Paul, Charlie and Mark. Middle row Judy and Marguerite, front, Steve and Tim.

Marilyn Burris 1937-2014

--by Sheila and Steve

In 1956 Edgar and Hazel Mason moved from West Warwick, Rhode Island to North Society Road in Canterbury so Edgar could start his own dairy farm. They had four children: Carolyn, Marilyn, Edgar III and Sheila. When the move took place, Edgar had to milk the cows in West Warwick in the morning, complete the move and then milk the cows that night in Canterbury.

The far end of North Society Road was a wonderful location, so peaceful and quiet. Old friends and relatives from Rhode Island would often come unannounced to visit the farm on Sunday afternoon and sit and talk for hours. Edgar started with 30 dairy cows and the farm grew to over 100. The farm Edgar and Hazel created is now the Tyler farm.

Marilyn had just graduated from high school and was able to get a job at Phillips Garage in Plainfield. She didn't have a license yet, so her mother had to drive her back and forth to work. She didn't know it at the time, but in the future, a customer there, Robert Manship, would become Canterbury's First Selectman and she would work with him as Canterbury's Town Clerk/Tax Collector.

She worked at Phillips garage for three years and then met her husband Richard Burris at the Baptist church in Danielson. He was from Oklahoma and was stationed at the Nike site in Foster, Rhode Island. They met in March and were married in October, moved to Danielson and eventually had two children, Richard and Susan. Marilyn got a job at the CBT bank and Richard worked second shift at Pratt & Whitney. It was later decided the whole family would move back to Canterbury so Richard could help Edgar with the farm work during the day.

Marilyn was then a stay-at-home Mom for twelve years, but after Richard died quite suddenly of cancer, leaving her a widow in 1971, she had to look for work.

At that time, Marguerite Simpson was the Canterbury Town Clerk; her assistant, Eunice Parker, left to take the job as secretary to the School Superintendent. Marguerite asked Marilyn to consider the assistant job; she accepted it and worked 5 hours a week.

After just two weeks as the new Assistant Town Clerk, Marilyn was on her own, as Mrs. Simpson had to have surgery and was out for two weeks.

Marilyn said, when faced with some situations she hadn't yet learned about, she just had to work her way through. This would become a pattern—whenever Marguerite was sick or on vacation, something unique would always come up that Marilyn had never handled before. Because Marguerite was so organized and kept such good records, Marilyn could always find a solution to any problem.

In her second year on the job, the Board of Assessors needed a clerk, so she took on that job as well. This was before computers and one of Marilyn's jobs was to hand-write the Grand List. The next year they needed someone on the Board of Assessors, so she ran for the job, was elected and served with Charles Savarese and Fred Dorr.

Marilyn said the Town saved a lot of money by electing her and Charles, because Charles was on disability with Social Security and Marilyn received a widow's pension so both could only receive a small amount of outside income.

Marguerite Simpson was a firm believer in education and Marilyn began to take certification classes for Tax Collection and Assessing. She was the first person in the State of Connecticut to be certified as an Assessor and Tax Collector She worked with Marguerite for 13 years as her Assistant and felt qualified to handle the job, so when Mrs. Simpson retired in 1985, Marilyn ran for the Canterbury Town Clerk/Tax Collector job and won the election. She would be the top vote getter for 7 elections.

Unlike Marguerite, who knew everyone in town, Marilyn missed growing up in Canterbury and felt she didn't have the advantage of knowing residents when they were younger. However, she called Canterbury her adopted home.

She dealt with a lot of people in this position and one

185

person she remembers was Joseph Kulaga who would drive his tractor from home on Cemetery Road, down to the old Town Office under the Dr. Helen Baldwin School to pay his taxes. He also sent her a congratulatory card when she won her first election.

She worked with current Assistant Town Clerk, Beth Heon, for fifteen years and hired Patricia Spruance, who was Town Clerk/Tax Collector for eight years and Natalie Cordes, the current Town Clerk/Tax Collector. Marilyn retired in January 2000, but couldn't stay away. She still worked four hours a week checking land records and sending documents back to land owners. As of July 1, 2008, her last day at work, Marilyn had worked for the Town of Canterbury for 36 years.

Her coworkers told me one of Marilyn's greatest qualities was her interest in others. She had a smile for every Canterbury citizen and truly cared about them and what was going on in their lives.

Marilyn was also involved in the Canterbury PTA. When she was asked to be a PTA officer she decided it was time to finally get her driver's license, so at 32 she took the courses and got her license.

Marilyn was invited to Calvary Chapel's "March to Sunday School in March" when her daughter was two years old and she's been going ever since, for over forty years. She was on the church's Board of Christian Education, Music Committee, Hospitality Committee, served as treasurer for the Sunday School and Women's Christian Fellowship and sang in the choir where she was a soloist.

Marilyn's faith sustained her through a series of tragedies in her life, as described further on in this article.

In her last years she came down with Parkinson's, which slowly robbed her of every ability; in her last year she could not do anything, not even talk. And yet she remained steadfast in her faith.

Because of her Parkinson's Disease, Marilyn had to spend her last years in a nursing home. There she

186

continued her godly and sweet life right to the end, being a blessing to all those around her.

Here are some pictures of Marilyn in grammar school and later with her children

Marilyn at her retirement party and at work in the town office

Following is an entry about Marilyn in my (Steve's) devotional book, *EDIFIED! 365 Devotionals to Stimulate Personal Worship and Spark Inner Transformation* (available at www.edifyingservies.com)

"Put on the whole armor of God so that when the day of evil comes you may be able to stand, and having done all, to stand."

At a prayer meeting in my home church, we were talking about a painful happening in someone's life when Marilyn spoke up to say, "Even in this we know that God is good and all He allows to come to us is good." Nice words, true words, easy to say, hard to live. But Marilyn knew what she was talking about.

When she was 32, her husband was diagnosed with cancer, and in nine months he was gone, leaving her with two small children to care for. She had to go to work and support her family, which she did very willingly.

Then several years later, one Sunday afternoon on the way to sing at a convalescent home, her car spun on some ice, hit a telephone pole and her beautiful, angelic teenage daughter was killed. Marilyn said that God gave her a peace from the moment of impact and she was able to let go of any self-blame or bitterness.

Other difficulties followed: a son who left the faith and made poor choices in life; a deer that totaled her car; a mother who got cancer and died a long and painful death; a father who became ill and as a diabetic had several amputations. She took care of them all to the end. Then she developed a serious, painful problem with her spine and yet remained sweet, trusting and full of praise. She met it all with genuine peace, acceptance and thanksgiving.

In her last years, she came down with Parkinson's Disease, which slowly robbed her of every ability; in her last year she could not do anything, not even talk. And yet she remained steadfast in her faith.

Her response to these human tragedies was the opposite of the psalmist who wrote, "When my heart was grieved and my spirit embittered, I was senseless and ignorant, I was a brute beast before you" (Ps. 73:21,22). He played the victim, while she chose the "more than a victor" role.

Why was Marilyn's response different? Because she was not willfully ignorant as the psalmist was (and as we are when we complain about things, forgetting the goodness and power of God). She had cultivated her first love for Jesus. She regularly spent time with God, worshiped Him and dwelt in the knowledge of His faithfulness.

In each difficulty, she reached out and took the grace that God offered. This sustained her, deepened her and caused her to bear lots of fruit for those around her, all of it tasty. You would have to look long and hard to find another person who is so genuinely sweet. Truth is pure and powerful when we live it.

Prayer: "Help me to take this example of Marilyn, Lord, to spend that time with you every day, learning to think like you, filling the cup of my soul with the beauty of your Truth so when the day of testing comes I will be ready to trust and praise you in all. Amen."

Malcolm Wibberley 1892-1960
--by Steve

Malcolm, my grandfather (here after referred to as "Grandpa"), was born in Canterbury, on Echoland Farm on Lisbon Road, in 1892.

His grandfather, William Wibberley, had come over

from England with his three brothers in the 1860s to work in the textile mills in Massachusetts. When William had saved up enough money, he bought the farm in Canterbury on Lisbon Road.

Grandpa's parents, Sam and Ann Janet (in picture on left), worked it some and cut timber on it.

Grandpa Sam was active in Canterbury, serving on the board of selectmen and being a founder and leader of Grange No. 70. However, his wife was not happy living in the primitive restrictions of the farm, so in 1912 they moved to Plainfield where the five children had attended high school. There Grandpa Sam pursued his hobby of raising flowers, which he shared with all his neighbors and friends.

When Malcolm graduated from high school in 1910, he was awarded a scholarship to Yale University in New Haven to study electrical engineering. His scholarship money was only enough for three years, so he accelerated his courses and graduated in 1913 (graduation picture on right) before his money ran out, an indication of his strength of character.

He took a job in Pittsburgh working for Westinghouse corporation, but was not happy in the big city, so after a year left and returned to Connecticut and farming.

First, he took a job in a large farm in New Britain where he learned about selective breeding and modern farming methods.

He married Jessie Sage of Norwich (picture here of the couple with the first three of their five children), bought Echoland Farm in Canterbury from his father and settled into the old farmhouse there.

The first mention of this house was in 1741 in the tax records, meaning that when Malcolm's grandfather bought the farm in the 1860s, the house was already at least 140 years old!

The farm was very rocky with limited fields available for raising hay. The pasture land across the road from the farm buildings had so many rocks that you could (and still can) easily cross it without ever having to step on the grass, as seen in the picture below taken in 1922 where Grandpa has his

niece sitting on a calf.

Those who had lived on the farm before Grandpa had done a lot of work in clearing fields and building stonewalls, and Grandpa and his children did more, removing rocks from hayfields and making new fields from woodlands. It was a never-ending task.

When Grandpa moved to Canterbury, his former employer had gifted him with a Guernsey bull of very good stock, and Grandpa began to build up his herd of registered Guernsey milk cows with this bull.

As time went on, Grandpa began to sell bottled milk and cream to neighbors, eventually going as far as Plainfield and Taftville. He also sold apples from the big orchard behind the barn and vegetables from his garden.

While busy in farming, he also took time for a number of other pursuits. One was electricity. Canterbury, as a whole, didn't have electricity until the 1940s (the Green area had it in 1929), but being an electrical engineer, by 1920 Grandpa was able to build his own electrical system.

He made a generator powered by a model T engine and supplemented it with batteries he made from large jars and lead plates, giving the family lights to work and read by.

He also had a keen interest in music and taught himself how to play thirteen different wind and percussion

instruments, including trumpet, clarinet, saxophone, baritone, trombone and drums. He then taught at least one of these to each of his five children, to many of his 22 grandchildren, as well as to neighbor children. In the picture on the left are his son Randy and daughter Elizabeth with their instruments in 1927.

Grandpa then formed a band that played for the Fourth of July celebration, grange meetings and other town events. On the right is a picture of Grandpa leading his marching band for the Fourth of July celebration in 1929. They are marching down route 14 and

are right the intersection with 169 on the Green.

Later he led a music program at Dr. Helen Baldwin School. He had me play whatever instrument he needed for the band, starting me on the base drum, then on the alto sax, tenor sax, clarinet, and trombone. I never mastered any of them, but dutifully fulfilled my role. In the picture below, Grandpa poses with his French horn and a student.

The many immigrant families in town looked to "Policeman Wibberley", as they called Grandpa, for help and guidance, which he gave whether they wanted it or not.

He would help them with getting a driver's license, or getting it back after an accident or drunk driving incident. He helped with property problems and other difficulties. One Finnish wife would call Grandpa whenever her husband would go on a drunken binge, and Grandpa would go up and play clarinet with him to calm him down.

When the old Russian up the street lost his wife and got a young woman to move in with him, Grandpa was soon at their door, telling them that they had to get married and took them to the Justice of Peace to tie the knot!

Grandpa was much involved in education in town, being chairman of the school board for many years. He was one of main forces behind building Dr. Helen Baldwin School,

thereby bringing the nine one room schools all together.

He would often tutor local students in Latin, Algebra and other courses, right up until shortly before he died.

In the picture on the left is Grandpa with his five children with their summer

193

haircuts: Randy, Max, Elizabeth, Janette and Ruth.

He also was a strong believer in having a two-party political system, so, in spite of being a strong Republican, when the Democratic party became weak, he joined it to successfully build it up. Thereafter some people called him "Mr. Democrat!"

He was involved in the Grange and was faithful in attending the Congregational Church on the Green. When someone who opposed him politically said he'd never attend church where Mr. Wibberley went, Grandpa said, "I'll not stand in the way of a man going to church; I'll go to the one in Lisbon!" and so he did.

There he taught Sunday School and one day startled his class by suddenly throwing down his book and jumping out the window. He'd noticed a car in the church parking lot rolling towards the road, so he ran to catch it, preventing a possible accident.

He was a very responsible person; if there was a need, he was ready to step up to meet it. In the

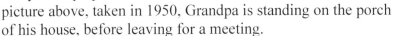

picture above, taken in 1950, Grandpa is standing on the porch of his house, before leaving for a meeting.

Near the end of his farming career, Grandpa sold his prize bull, Chancellor (in picture on left with Grandpa and Dad holding him), to a farm in Saudi Arabia for a sizable sum. True to his generous nature, he divided that windfall among his five children, all of whom were busy raising large families, so such a help was greatly appreciated.

I remember him as being quite stern, a hard worker who expected us all to work hard with him. But he was also generous, paying us kids for our work and very willing to help anyone he could.

 Here is a view of the farm in the mid-sixties.

In his 68th year he built a stand for the garbage barrels at the school, using oak boards cut from timber on his farm. A few weeks later in February of 1960, he suffered a massive heart attack and died saying, "It's too early, I have so much more I'd like to do!" But he had to leave it to the rest of us, and doing the chores for the eight cows he still had fell to me for the next four years.

Grandpa left a big hole in all of our lives, but better yet, he left a fine example of living out his faith with good deeds, responsibility, generosity, ingenuity, hard work and a love for music.

Here's a poem about him, written by his daughter, Elizabeth Wibberley Brown, in 1971, eleven years after Grandpa's death.

Yale '13
Electrical engineering
Short lived;
Westinghouse could survive
Without him,
But, without land,
He couldn't survive.
He felt
"close to earth"
Is close to God,"
So went back to the farm.
"My, my, a wasted College education!"
I'd hear the relatives say.

How could they say wasted?
It was ploughed into life
For enrichment;
Who can tell, in what way,
It may be nourishing still, today?
He was the third generation
On the same hundred acres,
And three more to come, so far.
Close to earth,
Close to God,
Close to family;
Where sons could see
What fathers do
And know what fathers are,
As they worked together
The season's harvest,
Aided or aborted by nature.
And in the house,
Jokes, puns and laughter,
Dickens aloud after dinner.
Each one with a horn
To play a part
Of the music in his band.
Who could fault such a home
On the land?
Poor in the destructible
Trinkets and treasures;
Rich in intangibles
Still multiplying
Beyond measure.

Malcolm and Jessie Wibberley in 1948 with some of their 22 grandchildren

Here is an article about Grandpa and Grandma that appeared in the Norwich Bulletin in 1925

Malcolm Wibberley is one who practices modern dairy methods and proves that brains and hard work overcome natural disadvantages.

It is safe to say that the State of Connecticut has no less promising agricultural sections than Canterbury where Malcolm is building up a dairy herd and wresting a living from a one-time abandoned farm. Farm homes are few in that particular district because the land is rough, most of it forested and the cleared land has rock ledges offering insurmountable obstacles to any but the stoudest-hearted farmer.

Any city chap who figures that the hardy spirit of the early pioneers is dead should visit the Wibberley farm. The road is long and rough and narrow and the farm itself is anything but pretentious. On this farm, however, Mr. and Mrs. Wibberley are making a living for themselves and five small children. And the dairy herd, though small, is a distinct credit to Windham county's dairy industry.

Mr. Wibberley was born on the farm he now operates, but he early decided that he wanted to be an electrical engineer so went to study at Yale. After graduation he went to Pittsburgh, PA, to work for a year in the big Westinghouse plant, but he longed for the country. He returned to Canterbury

for one season's work and then spent a year at a dairy and fruit farm in NH.

In the spring of 1916 he moved to the Mooreland Farm in New Britain, CT, where he worked for E. A. Moore, one of the leading breeders of Guernsey cattle in the country. Here he learned the importance of the quality of dairy cows and studied intensely the work of raising pure-bred cattle. After three years, Mr. Wibberley felt sufficiently confident to run a farm of his own. His father had abandoned the home place and was ready to turn it over to his son.

Mr. Moore gave him an imported Guernsey bull as a parting gift and, with this bull and five grade cows, Wibberley started his business. It was a formidable venture as the land was not fertile, the pasture land was largely grown up to brush, the buildings needed repair and capital was very limited.

As soon as he could Mr. Wibberley bought a registered Guernsey cow and began building a herd of high quality cows. Milk from his herd of eight cows is separated on the farm and the cream is sold in Plainfield at 90 cents a quart. Surplus skim milk is sold to neighbors who keep hens. Milk and butter fat records are kept and heifer calves are from the best producing cows are kept. The herd is now averaging over two hundred fifty pounds of butter fat annually. This is not as high as he would like but he doesn't yet have high quality feed for them. He is moving to change this, having seeded fields with alfalfa and clover and has put up a silo.

One good part of the farm is the apple orchard, having a hundred trees consisting of excellent varieties set out by Mr. Wibberley's father some thirty years ago. During his first winter on Echoland Farm Mr. Wibberley thoroughly pruned the trees and gave the orchard a good cleaning up. Since then spraying and fertilizing have been done regularly and some profitable crops of good quality fruit have been harvested.

The apples have been a great help while the dairy herd was becoming established and the fields being returned to a fertile condition. The fruit is retailed in the village of Plainfield, although many neighbors also come to buy Echoland Farm apples. Mrs. Wibberley makes apple sauce which finds a ready sale among the cream customers.

His first five years were difficult but Mr. Wibberley now has an excellent small herd, the buildings have been repaired, he has plenty of silage and this season he cut three crops of alfalfa from one field. With better feed, his cream sales ought to increase considerably and with a larger income he can add to his herd.

The Wibberleys give much credit for the recent success of the farm to Maurice Jacobs, the young man who has been with them the past year and a half as assistant herdsman and general helper; and to the neighbors who have helped with building and filling the silo and at other critical times. Even Mr. Wibberley's father, who is in his 70s, comes over from Plainfield to help at times.

To some people, the strangest part of this story is that the Wibberleys are native born Americans, showing that the race is not as "soft" as it has be advertised!

Maxwell S. Wibberley 1918-2006
--by Steve

My father, Max, was born in New Britain in 1918, the second of the five children of Malcolm and Jessie Wibberley. Most of his growing up years were spent on the Wibberley farm on Lisbon Road, known as Echoland Farm. There he learned to work hard and master many skills, including playing the trumpet.

At age four he accompanied his older brother, Randy, to the one room school house on Route 169 at the end of Gooseneck Hill Road. Randy didn't want to go alone on the walk of about 3.5 miles each way through the woods, so Dad went with him. Dad said he'd be tuckered out by the afternoon and Lucy Hansen, who was in the 8th grade, would put him down on a back bench for a nap, covering him with her coat.

Dad and his siblings began doing chores early, as there was never an end to work needing to be done on the farm. One of Dad's chores was watering the work horses.

When he was about six, as he was leading the horses to the watering trough, one of them leaned down and bit him right across the face. Dad said he cried for two days and finally his father said. What can I get you to help you stop crying?" Dad answered, "A pony!"

So, Grandpa got him one, and he and Randy enjoyed riding it to school. In the picture above, Dad, much later in life, is leading the work horses out in front of his house.

Having started school early, Dad graduated from Plainfield high school when he was only 16. Taking after his father, he was the valedictorian, meaning he had to give a speech.

However, when the time came during the graduation ceremony, he was overcome with panic and rushed off the stage. When the family got home, his stern father didn't say a word about that failure, but gave him a gift of five dollars—a lot of money in 1936!

Dad and his siblings all followed his older brother, Randy, to Blackburn College in Illinois, a two-year school (as did my sister and several of my cousins). One main reason they all went there is that Blackburn had very low tuition and living costs because the students did all the work, including running the school's farm and doing all the construction.

Dad was very much at home with this type of set up and did well. He told of how one day he was assigned to clean out the liquid manure pit by the barn, so he "borrowed" his roommate's clothes, and returned them full of aroma.

He also ran track and cross country there and made some good friends that later proved significant in his life.

He used various means of transport to get back and forth to Blackburn from Connecticut: bus, hitchhiking and driving an old Ford. When he drove back after graduating, he was stopped by the police in Indiana who wanted to see his driver's license. Dad just pointed to the Illinois license plate and the police waved him on. Illinois didn't require or issue driver's licenses at the time.

Back home he worked on the farm before continuing his education. Below he's using a bull to pull a stone drag.

UConn was Dad's next stop. He was on the track team and joined a fraternity. As part of his fraternity initiation, he was driven some 30 miles from the campus at night and put out of the car to find his own way home. No problem for a farm boy who had hitchhiked all the way to Illinois and back several times.

He studied French, thinking he could become a teacher, but after graduating, went back into farming—which was a good thing for all the students he would have had; Dad had little patience for details. He was better at leading a bull in clearing a field (as in the picture above) than leading a classroom of uninterested students!

WW II was starting up, but Dad was turned down by the service, because he'd had hepatitis and also because he was a farmer, much needed to produce food for the country.

 He got a job at a big farm in Middle Town, along with his good friend, Dave Syme. In the picture on the left Dave, in foreground and Dad, in back were doing spring plowing on that farm.

As he was now 24, Dad began to think about getting married. He went through the list of all the girls he knew, and settled on one he'd met at Blackburn, Virginia Haslip.

He bought a bus ticket and went out to East St. Louis for a five-day visit. At the end of it, he asked her to marry him, something she wasn't expecting. She said she'd think about it for two weeks and let him know. His friend, Dave, said Dad was pretty difficult to get along with during those two weeks.

My mother said she couldn't make up her mind, and finally decided that if she had enough money in her pocket to send Max a telegram, she'd marry him—and she did.

Dad asked her when she'd like to marry and she said early August; being a city girl, she had no way of knowing that was right in the middle of haying season. But Dad agreed, got the time off and on August 3, 1942 they were married in East St. Louis. Then they immediately took a train back to Connecticut.

At the stop in Indianapolis, my mother's old boyfriend got on the train, and seeing Mom and Dad, was really surprised. "Hey, kids, what are you doing here?" he asked.

"We just got married!" my father replied.

"Oh...." The old boyfriend was obviously chagrined.

When he left, my mother said she went to the ladies' room and cried for an hour, got over it, then came out and went on with her new life. The picture above here is of Mom and Dad soon after they were married.

After meeting Dave Syme, my mother decided to introduce him to her good friend Kay, and shortly they, too, were married and remained life-long friends with my parents.

Dave soon moved to Hilly Land Farm in Scotland. And Dad moved to North Stonington to work with his brother Randy who was managing a farm for the owner of the velvet mill there.

Even though Dad was only making about $800 a year as a farm hand, he managed to buy a new Studebaker car (at left with us three kids). The very modern design

brought some ridicule, people asking which was the front and which the back. Dad really enjoyed cars and would purchase a new one every three or four years, buying only Studebakers until the company went out of business.

Our favorite was the 1954 Hawk, (in picture above) one of the earliest cars to have fins and a sporty look.

While living in Stonington, Dad and Mom had the first two of their five children, and shortly after I was born, moved to Canterbury to work with Grandpa on the farm. Together Dad and Grandpa continued the never-ending task of picking rocks off the fields, as well as burying stone walls and clearing land for more fields.

Dad was ever thinking about more ways to increase his income. He bought a small bulldozer in the early 50s (in the picture below I'm sitting on it as a six-year-old) using it on the farm to clear land, but also doing custom work for others.

However, after he backfilled a cement block foundation and cracked it, he decided bulldozer work was not the way for him to go.

He next tried selling farm equipment, but that didn't go too well, either.

Then he stumbled onto what was to be his next career, selling tires. He needed a set of tires for his truck and found an ad in a magazine for just what he wanted at a really good price. When a neighbor saw his new tires, he asked Dad to get him some, too and the business began. He officially launched "Tires for Less" in 1952 with a sales tax certificate he got for $1. The picture above shows Dad at a booth he had to advertise his business at the Brooklyn Fair.

Dad first worked out of our house cellar, quickly expanding from truck tires to car and farm tires, and getting a franchise for Armstrong Tires. In the picture above, all of us kids are standing in front of Dad's service truck parked by the cellar.

Since he was still a full-time farmer, we kids were often called upon to help facilitate his tire business; this started when I was 6. If a customer came during milking time, I had to take over for Dad so he could wait on the customer.

I could barely reach the vacuum line to plug in the milking machine, and had a hard time lugging the full milk buckets to the milk cans, but soon was adept at it. Other times we pitched in with jacking up cars, taking off the wheels and changing the tires.

About 1958 Connecticut passed new laws regulating the dairy industry; one requirement was that the cows had to be kept in a concrete-floored building. To comply would have been more than either Grandpa or Dad wanted to invest, so Grandpa retired at 66 and Dad went full time with his tire business.

Then when Grandpa died suddenly in 1960, Dad moved the business from the cellar to the cow barn. We still had eight cows, so we'd be changing tires after school, then when a break came, I'd go in the back and milk the cows. Note in the picture on the left the truck tires behind me and my cohort of cats, including the one on my lap, waiting for some milk to drink.

Road calls were another aspect of the business that were both challenging and fun. Sometimes Dad would take us on night calls and we'd hold the flashlight for him while he worked fixing a truck flat or a tractor tire.

Eddie Vaclavick was one of the customers we'd visit, and he and Dad became very good friends. In fact, Dad was on good terms with most everyone. One of his sayings was, "Don't let politics or business get in the way of friendships," and he lived that having good friends both with Democrats and Republicans, even when things were tense politically in town.

He had a lot of sayings, like, "Never refuse legitimately offered money--or anything else." Notice the word "legitimate" there. He often said, "Work with gravity, not against it." It's amazing how often I find myself doing the opposite, but even today his words come to mind and I heed them.

Another was, "Money is not important at all—if you have enough of it." And "Pay attention to what's going on around you—it can save you a lot of time and money." This certainly was true, such as noting the new sound the milking machine vacuum pump was making alerted us to it being low on oil.

All through his life, even with two full time jobs, Dad  kept up with his trumpet playing and would take us along with him to play in the East Woodstock Silver Cornet Band. This also meant we played at the Brooklyn and Woodstock Fairs each year, getting in free and spending considerable time there.

In the picture above, Dad plays a duet with his grandson. Dad played for over sixty years, right up until the end of his seventies, and for the last twenty of those years he continued to take lessons to improve himself, practicing every day.

Dad tried to expand his business with a wholesale route, but in the end, it seemed we lost more than we gained. However, the retail business more than made up for it and continued to grow through the years. Dad's philosophy of was, "Sell a good product at a good price and stand behind it." That made loyal customers and gave us a lot of free advertising.

Once I accidentally warped the front rotors of a customer's car by tightening the wheel nuts unevenly, and when he came back to complain about it, we immediately repaired them for free. That customer was a barber and for the next 40 years he told his customers what a great place Max Wibberley had.

Dad was generous and, like his father, was willing to help others out. After Dad died, a number of people told me how, when they were financially strapped, Dad would fix a flat, or come out and repair a tire, or sell them a new one, saying, "Pay me when you can."

Dad also drew customers with his ability to entertain them. He was an enthusiastic story teller, especially after getting involved with motorcycles. He could talk so fast that more than one customers asked me if he was speaking English!

Sometimes he'd get out his trumpet and play for them. Then we also had a troop of pets, including, cats, kittens, dogs

and a pet raccoon that would entertain the customers.

Our shop (left) was pretty primitive, with no waiting room and no bathroom, and we worked out in the weather. But people enjoyed the good prices, the good products and the unusual

surroundings, so they kept coming back. We had customers that came from Rhode Island, Massachusetts, Vermont and New Hampshire, especially for tractor tires.

In 1964 I went off to college in Pennsylvania and my brother, Les left for school a year later. Dad had to hire some help and his first employee was Harry Thurlow who worked for Dad for

207

a number of years. He was followed by others like Harry Baum (in the picture to the above, working with Dad to change a truck tire), Gary and Lenny Edmonds, Rene Beauchene, Ricky Miller and Brian Hill.

While at college I made a decision that changed Dad's life: I bought a motorcycle and rode it home from college in May of 1967. Dad made me sell it because it was, he said, so dangerous, but not before trying it out himself--and unbeknownst to me, he was hooked.

When I came home from college my senior year, I found Dad the proud owner of a new BSA 250 road bike. He quickly began to take it off road and eventually broke its transmission, so he got himself a BSA 440, a big, heavy off-road enduro bike. I bought the 250 BSA from him, had it repaired and rode it to Alaska, where I taught school in an Eskimo village on an Island sixty miles off the coast of Siberia--but that's another story, told in my book *From Canterbury to the Ends of the Earth and Back*. This is available in the Canterbury library.

After his father's death, Dad had been struggling with a midlife crisis and facing his mortality. Motorcycles became the way for him to regain excitement about life and to hang

onto his youth. He said that riding bikes brought on his second childhood, which was much more fun than the first one because now he had money!

He soon got into competition, first with enduros and then motocross. That's him in the picture above, number 95. He also tried to turn this new passion into another facet of his business. He set up a bike shop, got some minor brand franchises, and began selling bikes and parts.

He sponsored Gary Edmonds in enduro racing and

Gary went on to become a three-time gold medalist in the world championships. But the businesses never did make a profit and we finally auctioned everything off.

Dad continued with motocross and was a founding member of the Central Cycle Club. His enthusiasm for motorcycles and racing was immediately obvious to anyone who met him, for he talked of them incessantly. He traveled the whole of the New England area, entering motocross races, competing mostly against riders one third his age.

Being well over 50, his reflexes were not as good as the younger riders, but if it rained he would win, because he the skills to stay up in the mud.

In this pursuit of staying young, he had multiple accidents and broke a lot of bones in the process. This resulted in the leadership of the tire business falling to me, which I didn't mind at all.

In 1979, after running the business for ten years, I left the USA to live and work in the Middle East for the next 33 years. I gave my portion of the tire business to my younger brother, Sam, who eventually moved it to Dayville, and recently sold it to Town Fair Tire.

Finally, at age 63 Dad realized he couldn't keep up anymore and that his motocross days were over. So, he switched to running and bicycle racing. He ran many races, often winning his class. He even went to France to run in a race in Paris. And everywhere he went, Dad made friends. He was really an entertainer at heart, and his enthusiasm and quick speech won people over--or simply amazed them. He was not hard to remember.

Now that Dad was basically retired from the tire business, he turned his attention to the farm and began cutting and selling fire wood. He also started redoing fields, digging out or burying the big rocks that remained. He really put his life into the land. He had fun buying and running new and larger equipment.

Dad was, to put it mildly, a tough character with a high pain threshold and a fast healing rate. Here are several stories of his accidents that show this.

One summer evening after a full day of working in the

tire shop, I was taking a bath when I heard a loud "whuuump!" I immediately knew what it was: a truck tire had exploded. I threw on some clothes and ran barefoot to the shop to find Dad laying on the ground, his leg all bloodied.

He'd been pounding on a tire stuck on a truck and the ring had blown off, propelled by a crushing 100 pounds of air pressure. Fortunately, he was standing to the side and the ring struck his leg rather than hitting his head or chest, which would have killed him. His leg should have been cut off, but his heavy work pants gave just enough protection so, instead of severing it, his lower bone was just broken into twenty or so pieces.

Gary Edmonds drove him to the hospital in his van, while in the back I held his leg to keep it from flopping too much. The doctor put a cast on him from his toes to his hip, but as soon as we got home, Dad cut off the top part of the cast down to the knee so he could ride his bicycle!

In his follow-up visits to the doctor there was no sign of healing. Finally, the doctor said he'd give it another month, but if nothing happened, then he was going to have to do bone grafts. My four siblings and I knew that would be very hard for Dad, so we all prayed for healing.

I added a little prayer of unbelief, "Lord, if you are going to heal him, have his next appointment be postponed." And just as Dad was going out the door to that appointment, the phone rang. It was the nurse saying that the doctor had an emergency and could Max come tomorrow instead?

Well, I determined I was going to go with him and see this answer to prayer. After x-rays were taken, the doctor came out with one in his hand. He held it up to the light and said, "Max, you must know the Man upstairs. Your breaks are almost fully healed. I've never seen anything like this in my life!"

Dad acknowledged that this was a miracle, an answer to prayer, God working directly in his life, but he still preferred to have God five miles down the road, just close enough for help, but far enough away so as to not interfere. Dad liked being independent.

Some years later when his left hand began to atrophy;

the doctor told him that a nerve was pinched but that an operation could correct it.

As Dad asked questions, the doctor told him his hand would have to be in a cast for up to six months and that he wouldn't be able to play his trumpet the whole time. Dad said he couldn't possibly be away from trumpet playing for that long, so he decided not to have the operation; he would ignore his problem.

Shortly after that, while practicing for motocross out in the field, he hit a woodchuck hole and did an endo which broke his left hand. The doctor put a cast on it, and when Dad got home, he cut off enough so he could play his trumpet. When the cast came off after 4 weeks, the atrophied part of his hand had recovered on its own! Seems that the break had cured the pinched nerve: therapy by motocross.

Dad had a log splitter that was shaped like a huge screw attached directly to the power-take-off of his tractor. He would roll a log up to it and push it against the sharp, turning point of the splitter, which would then pull the wood onto itself and split it.

One cold winter day, he got too close and the giant screw caught his pant leg. It threw Dad around and around, knocking him out. When he woke, his pants were gone, ripped off by the splitter and he had a huge burn on his inner thigh where the screw had twisted his pant leg. Dad just got up and, without any pants, walked home in the freezing wind!

Another time he was clearing the land where Manship Park is now, and as he finished cutting a log, the tip of the saw dropped and cut into the top of his foot. It, of course, bled badly, but Dad just calmly shut off his saw, climbed into his big F750 Ford and drove himself to the walk-in clinic in Plainfield.

Years later I was working in the tire shop one day when, shortly before lunch, I saw Dad walking down the lane. He looked odd and was cradling one arm. I ran to meet him and saw that his face was bloody and his eyes looked strange.

"You'd better take me to the hospital," he said.

I helped him into the car and we roared off. On the way, he told me what had happened. He had cut down a tree

211

growing on the edge of the woods, but, since it had many large branches growing out towards the light, it didn't fall completely to the ground, but rested on those out stretched branches.

Dad had begun cutting off the long branches so he could get to the main trunk. As He was working, the tree suddenly rolled and he was struck on the head by a large branch he didn't see coming. It hit with such force that it crushed the front of his skull, knocking him to the ground and hurting his arm. Since the bones around his eyes were broken, one eye was looking upwards and the other downwards.

The average person would have been knocked out and probably would not have survived such a serious accident, but Dad was such a tough old Yankee that he didn't even lose consciousness. Instead, he got up, shut off his chain saw and walked home in the 95-degree heat, climbing over two stone walls on the way!

When we got to the emergency room, the doctor called in a facial specialist. As this doctor was examining him, Dad asked him, "Are you going to have to operate on my face?"

"Yes, I'll have to lift off your whole face and wire all those bones back together," replied the doctor.

"Well, when you're done will I be able to play the piano?" Dad asked.

"Why certainly," said the doctor.

"Great," said Dad, "I could never play it before!"

The doctor laughed and shook his head, "Well, we've got no problem with spirit here, do we?" he commented.

This past week, May of 2017, 45 years later, I saw that doctor, and he remembered Dad's joke!

That was Dad-- when others would have been totally incapacitated, he was cracking jokes. [This story is a quote from my book *From Canterbury to the Ends of the Earth and*

Back, available in the Canterbury Library]

Dad continued to ride his motorcycle and run until his 81st year when he began having small strokes, probably the result of the many concussions he'd had, both in racing and in cutting firewood.

When he had his first larger stroke, Dad's personality changed. Most people I knew who were incapacitated with a stroke became unhappy, impatient and sometimes bitter. With Dad, it was the opposite. He went from being basically an 81-year-old teenager—self-absorbed, unthankful and thoughtless of others--to being quiet, thoughtful and thankful. This was wonderful both for him in his new restricted state and for my older sister, Andrea, who cared for him and my mother at home for the next four years.

As Mom descended into Alzheimer's, she began to talk about how she was going to go to heaven because she was a good person. And if you wanted to compare her to almost anyone else, she would register in the top one percent of fine people. She had faithfully attended Calvary Chapel and had, for over 30 years, taught the beginning Sunday School class; most of the young adults in the church had been her students. She had also been the librarian for many, many years. She was a good person, behind the scenes quietly doing kind and supportive things for many people.

We were all convinced she was born again and on her way to heaven because she had accepted Christ as her Savior, especially after she was baptized at age 52. However, now here she was, declaring it was her own goodness that would get her to heaven. Alzheimer's makes you so honest!

My sister, Andrea, tried to reason with her, but Mom was firm. Then Andrea got out a booklet that Mom's father had given her. He had been much like Mom, a very good person, a faithful member of the Methodist church, even being the chairman of the evangelism committee for many years. But in his early 70s he had finally understood the gospel, that he was a sinner unable to save himself and had to instead surrender to Christ, trusting him to save him. And after making that decision, my grandfather became a real evangelist, sharing with many about his new born-again faith.

Mom took that little booklet her father had used to share his faith and read it; then she said, "If this is what my father believed, then I'm ready to pray!" She prayed with Andrea to accept Christ as her Savior and put her hope in His finished work rather than her own goodness.

And she changed! At her stage of Alzheimer's, she had a hard time going to Michael's grocery store, but she declared she now wanted to go to St. Louis to visit her older sister! So Andrea bought tickets and took her there.

Our aunt Hazel was also a good person who had never wanted to hear about her need for a Savior. But now she was bed ridden in a nursing home, unable to do anything for herself. As Andrea visited, she asked Aunt Hazel if she would like to accept Christ as her Savior--and she replied in a strong voice, "Yes!" So they prayed together. After Andrea returned to Canterbury, she got a letter from Aunt Hazel's care taker who asked, "What did you do to your aunt? She was so different after you were here!" What happened is that Aunt Hazel was born again and began her eternal life with God's Spirit entering into her. She died three weeks later a happy woman.

So our family has had a record of being stubbornly independent, relying on our own goodness and ability to cope, until finally seeing reality. As I've mentioned, this was true for Dad, too. And he had yet to come to an understanding of his need for God's help.

Dad eventually reached the point where he could no longer walk, as in the picture here with my son, Josh. So, my sister, who was also caring for my mother who had Alzheimer's, could no longer care for him at home. She and her husband moved my parents to Columbus,

Ohio where my brother Les, and my sister, Marcia lived.
There they found a nice nursing home and put Mom and Dad
in it. Andrea, was there every day for 6 to 8 hours to care for
them, as well as everyone else on their wing; and my other
siblings came often.

After seeing Dad incapacitated, lying in his bed in the
nursing home, my wife, Barbara, wrote the following poem
about Dad, giving a quick overview of his life..

The Old Farmer's Hands
These hands once held
The pitchfork and the spade
They gathered rocks
And threw them on a cart

They handled saw
And steering wheel
Milked cows
And played the trumpet well.

Working with tires
Made them black
 And
The fingers got so gnarled

And now those working hands
Lie clean
and useless
On a spotless sheet

Sometimes they touch
The wheel chair spokes
And little grand
children's hair

The rocky soil
These hands
once wrestled with
Is also lying still.

My mother died a few months later, and the day after, Dad had another stroke that affected his speech: he could no longer speak intelligibly, and the doctor said he also could not understand. But, periodically he would open up and be able to interact well for an hour or so, then close up again.

Dad had never had much interest in spiritual things. He went to church for the social aspect, but was glad to have God far enough away so as not to interfere. Dad wanted to be masculine, meaning he didn't need to ask anyone for help, including God. But his growing incapacity was making him face reality.

One day when my brother-in-law came to visit him, Dad was busy reading his Bible. "I don't want to visit, I want to read this," he insisted, "It's important!" So, my brother-in-law read with him for half an hour and they prayed together. Something was going on with Dad.

Then about a month later he again had an "open time" when he could speak and understand. He asked my sister to read to him some from the New Testament and they talked about Dad's table mate who had recently died. Then my sister asked Dad if he'd like to accept Jesus as his Savior, and he said, "Yes!" So, they prayed, and even in his limited condition, Dad changed. He lived two years more and died at 88, peaceful and content to go. A great end to a life lived to the full.

HATS OFF TO *Max*

Maxwell Sage Wibberley
July 11, 1918 – September 24, 2006

Part of his obituary read, "With his infectious laugh, rapid-fire conversation and generous nature, Max remains in the minds of many who recall his relentless pursuit of almost any activity that kept him going and running and racing. During the latter part of his life a rare brain disease deprived him of the use of his legs and speech, but did not diminish his spirit. And now we will see him again, in the presence of the Lord, running and racing and talking up a storm!"

Merritt Hawes   1899-1973
--by Steve

Merritt was a long-term resident of Canterbury. His father,

Hiram Hawes, (picture on left) moved here in 1909 and set up a water powered shop to manufacture his famous and fine fly rods (picture above on right). This building is still standing on Kitt Brook near the Quinnebaug Farm.

His grandfather, Hiram Leonard, who was a gunsmith and professional hunter, hunted moose and caribou to sell to lumber camps back in 1850s. He was also an avid fisherman, which led him to invent a special wood beveler to triangulate split bamboo pieces in decreasing size, leaving the tips thin and supple. He then proceeded to invent the six-piece casting rod, by skillfully binding six triangulated pieces together to create rods with exquisite flexibility

When electricity came to the Green area where the Hawes lived, Hiram moved his shop to the barn behind his house. This building is still standing today, shown in picture here on right.

After his father died in 1929, Merritt and his mother continued the production of these fly-fishing rods, which are still highly prized today. During the second World War, they gave up the business.

Alton Olomarski bought two Hawes-made salmon rods and four trout rods. He said that Merritt's rods were even better than his father's.

You can look up Hiram Hawes rods online and find lots of information on them. Here's a little write up from one of the entries: "The rod itself it sports lovely pot-belly style ferrules and hand-turned cap and ring hardware. Naturally, it has the classic Hawes-style grip which tapers larger toward the front. The slide band sits on a white cedar spacer."

Another fly fishing enthusiast wrote, "What records...that I have, show that The Hawes tapers were ahead of their time. Wes Jordan stated that of all the early rod builders, Hawes was the best. I have a 7' taper that Elsie Hawes gave me that ranks with the best."

Another commented, "Every Hawes I've cast has been a beauty, and the detailing has been magnificent."

Prices today for these beautiful rods are $1500 or more; in 1913 an 8 footer sold for $50!

Merritt, like his father, mother and grandfather, was also a champion caster, as this article in a fishing magazine tells. "Merrit Hawes of Canterbury, CT was one of the first New England casters to become a member of the Hundred Footers Club . He is a very skillful caster, and the only one that I know of in New England who has competed in the national tournaments. His moderate ways, good sportsmanship, and agreeable manners are always noticeable.

"Fly fishing and casting for Merritt seem more of a second nature than acquired arts! He is the third generation to carry out this form of sport, as he is the grandson of Hiram

219

Leonard, who invented the six-strip bamboo rod, and the son of the late W. H. Hawes, whose name will be recalled by many as one of the greatest fly casters of the country.

"Should you chance to visit his home, there you will see quantities of silver cups, medals and prizes won by Hawes Club members and fly fishermen should not pass up the opportunity of meeting Merritt Hawes. His knowledge of casting and fishing rods will enlighten the most critical user." To the right is a picture  of a silver cup Hiram Hawes won in a New York tournament.

Jeff Smith, his grandson, said Merritt was quiet, very gentlemanly in a Victorian sense. He was influenced by his grandmother for whom all had to be proper, teaching him that manners were very important.

Merit was an avid Harley Davidson rider and, as I  remember him, had the big belt buckle to go with it.

In this picture Merritt (on the left) sits on his Harley in front of this house with his good friend, Doug Dean. Doug, unfortunately, died in his mid-20s of some unknown illness.

After his father died, Merritt and his mother continued to produce those beautiful rods until he got a job working for the State Highway Department. He continued to repair rods until about 1950.

He was also a avid hunter, especially of foxes, as seen here in this picture below.

Like most people in Canterbury, Merritt had a horse whom he named Harry. He had to put in hay to feed Harry through the winter. In this picture he's gathering hay from the fields around his house with help from Harry.

Merritt was one of the founding members of the Volunteer Fire Department and the fire truck was kept in his barn until the fire house was built.

He was the Fire Chief for years, and was active in the Fire Department right to the very end of his life.

When Calvary Chapel and its new addition burned, he was there to lead the effort to put out the fire, although the fire had too much of a head start to save anything.

Afterwards he wisely suggested to the pastor, Mr. Strube, that he put out a collection box so all the people who came to see the smoldering ruins could contribute to rebuilding. The money put into that box paid for all the costs of putting in the new cellar which was capped and used by the church until the new upper structure was completed two years later.

After he retired from the State road crew, Merritt began growing gladiolas in two large fields behind his

house, and sold them to Domicos Greenhouse in Jewett City. In this picture Merritt sits in his back yard with his two dogs.

Alton Olomorski related how, when he was working one day on the road in front of the church on the Green, Merritt came over to talk and told him that he just found out he had terminal cancer.

In the summer of 1972 Merritt started going downhill and died in April of 1973. As was fitting for a long-term Fire Chief, his casket was carried from the funeral home to Cary Cemetery on the fire truck.

One last picture taken in from of the Hawes house when Route 169 was being rebuilt before paving.

Michael Pappas
--by Steve

There has been a store at the Canterbury Green for many years and all the owners had their store in the same building in the picture below.

Above, Frank Hoxsie is the one who constructed this building for his store on the green; it was also the post office.

Later it was the Frink and Wright store, seen above.

Then it was the Romanoff's turn. Above are Bill and his son Bob out in front of their store.

When Bill decided to go fulltime into his orchid business, he sold the store to Michael Pappas.

I remember well going into this store when it was "Michael's" with my mother. The meat section was at the back, and we'd go back there first. It was a homey and comfortable place. Michael knew every customer by name and it certainly was the place to shop in those days.

As his business grew, Michael bought the lot across the street and built a modern, spacious building that today is the IGA Store.

In the picture, here on the left, is the grand opening ceremony for Michael's new store, with first selectman Ed Wasco cutting the ribbon. From left to right, Michael, his mother, Helen, Ed, and Michael's wife, Georgette. Michael went on to open several other stores, including one in Jewett City, and one in the Danielson area.

Miller Family

--by Sheila, Donna Miller and Steve

When I (Sheila) attended Dr. Helen Baldwin School, the students were always arranged alphabetically and I sat next to Joseph Miller all through grade school. I was a cheerleader with Darlene Miller. Elmer Miller was my bus driver for all twelve years of school. Recently, I talked with Dorothy S. Miller who told me some of the Miller family history.

Her husband's grandfather, Paul Miller, was born in Northeastern Germany, an area bordered by Poland and Russia, which annexed the section where his family lived, and they were driven out, suffering greatly.

His mother somehow saved enough to send Paul over to America to save him from further hardship and give him a chance for a new start. She also gave him a new set of clothes telling him to put them on when he saw the Statue of Liberty, and to throw his old clothes away.

He arrived in New York in about 1900 at age 17, alone and unable to speak English. He seemed to have been watched over from above, as he got help from a number of people and ended up in a German settlement on Long Island. There he met and married his wife, Frieda and became a baker, even having his own bakery. However, he had a desire to be a farmer and raise crops, so he began looking for a farm.

He was thinking about going to Georgia and being a peanut farmer, or to New England to raise vegetables. Since it

was closer, he came to Canterbury to look at what is now the Dean farm on Cemetery Road, but decided against it.

On the way back home he spotted a piece of land on what is now Miller Road. In the picture here are the remains of the house on the property. It reminded him of the farm he grew up on when he lived in Germany, especially Little River that bordered the property. Although it took

225

several years, he was finally able to purchase it in 1922.

He moved his family into an old ten-room farmhouse built in 1790. They had no trouble filling the house since the Millers had nine children by the time they moved to Canterbury and went on to have a total of ten, six of whom are in the picture below.

Above are, back row, left to right, Edward, parents Frieda and Paul, Joe, Front row, Fredrick, George, Robert, and Elmer. Not pictured are the three eldest, Henry, Paul, and Dorothea, and the youngest, Ann.

The Miller Road section of Canterbury was a great place to raise children, with wide open spaces and lots of activities in the crystal clear water of Little River, with swimming, boating and fishing in the summer and skating and sliding in the winter.

There was lots of work to be done - planting vegetables, bringing them to market, raising chickens and pigs and milking the cows. They were industrious workers and as a result, during the depression they had plenty to eat.

One factor in their farming success was the proximity of the river: they always had enough to water their gardens. In the first years, all the water for house, gardens and animals had to be carried in buckets from the river. At one point Pop broke his arm so the boys had to do all the water hauling. They secretly wondered if he didn't break his arm on purpose so he would get out of that duty!

There were three water-powered mills in the Miller's neighborhood that made lumber, hoops and coffins. The coffin mill manufactured its own fabric to line the coffins. One local woman used this fabric to make her wedding dress.

The coffin mill was primarily a sawmill and in addition to coffins, made railroad ties from the chestnut trees which were plentiful in Canterbury at the time.

Paul took advantage of this, cutting and selling timber to the mill. He had a horse named Dolly, who was trained to haul the logs to the mill on her own. Paul or his boys would hitch a log to Dolly's harness, give her a slap and off she would go down the hill to the mill. Someone there would unhitch the log, put the chains up on her collar, give her a slap, and off she would go back up the hill.

 A step dam was created for the mills and you can still see part of the structure today and the massive stones used to create it, as shown in this picture. This dam was washed out in the Hurricane of '38. It was rebuilt, but was washed out again the next year.

Eventually, the lumber mill was taken down and the Millers used the materials to build a garage on the other side of the road across from their house.

The town built a bridge across the Little River in front of the Miller's house and Paul's son, Robert, was sure this would wash away, too, since, when they were children, the river would flood and the water used to lap the bottom of the bridge floor. They were afraid to cross it when that happened.

The Miller children walked to Gayhead School (the house on the corner of Gayhead and Water Street) dreading the first day, because their Pop (Paul) would go with them to advise the teacher, that if the children misbehaved at school and were punished, they would also be punished at home.

Their teacher did send a note home one day, complaining that his two oldest sons, Henry and Paul, were speaking German with each other during class. Pop told them in no uncertain terms, "No more German in school. We are in America, we will speak English!" He followed up on this by not teaching his younger children German.

Since it was a one-room schoolhouse with all eight grades, the older children often taught the little ones and the teacher and the older boys had to maintain the stoves and arrange for drinking water.

On a warm spring day, the Miller children would hide their shoes in a nearby stonewall and go barefoot to school. There were separate outhouses for boys and girls. I'm sure the bathroom visits were shorter in the winter.

Some of their neighbors included the Binghams, the Olsons, the Deans, and Laurie Protcuk. Laurie had been captain of the last Russian Czar's personal body guard. He had been able to escape when the Bolshevik Revolution occurred and ended up in Canterbury where there were many other Russians.

After completing school, the Miller children worked at odd jobs until they were old enough for full time employment. Six of the Miller children built homes in Canterbury, raised their children, living here the rest of their lives. Of the original family members, only Elmer and Frederick are still living today.

Millers in the Military

During the Second World War, Henry was drafted in August of 1941, and Joe, Elmer and George all followed. George became a Military Policeman, while Joe was in the combat infantry. For his training, he was in a number of Army camps in the US, the last one being in Texas (see picture on left). There, while in simulated combat training, he was crawling up a hill on his belly when he came

228

face to face with a rattle snake. Reacting quickly, he whipped off his helmet, slammed it down over the snake and retreated. That quick-thinking ability probably helped keep him alive in all that lay before him.

He fought his way all across Africa, up into Sicily and on up the boot of Italy. His weapon was initially a 1903 Springfield rifle, but he shot it so much that the barrel wore out. He was then issued a 1917 Springfield, but he didn't like it because it "kicked like a mule" and wasn't accurate.

 In addition to being an infantryman, Joe was trained as a demolitions expert, and would be called in to blow up defenses, concertina wire and barriers.

Joe (standing in picture on the left) said combat in Italy was fierce, as the Germans were determined to hold them off. As the Americans advanced, the Germans simply retreated to the next ridge and made the Americans pay dearly to take each one.

Near the end of the war, Joe was knocked unconscious in battle. The clean-up crew picked him up for dead and threw him into a truck full of bodies. He woke up to find himself among all the corpses. Newt Bingham said that this happening, along with his years of frequent combat, left him with a tremor that made it hard for him to even light a cigarette when he returned to Canterbury.

Elmer followed Joe all through Africa up into Italy, but he had a different assignment, collecting all the equipment left on the field after a battle—guns, machine guns, bayonets and other weapons—and to get them refurbished and redistributed to those going into further combat. He also, at times, had to help collect the dead.

Elmer said he could tell when another battle was coming because bulldozers would dig a big long trench; then Italian prisoners would dig individual graves at the bottom of it for all those who would be killed in the battle. He saw terrible things that aren't often mentioned in history books.

According to one source, Elmer and Joe (in picture on right) were able to meet up with each other in Italy.

Interestingly, this coincidence was repeated one generation later when Joe's two sons, Henry and Norman, met up in Bagdad (picture on left) when both were doing six-month duty tours in Iraq with the Air Force National Guard. More on that later.

Elmer had pictures of a number of things he saw in Italy, including the tower of Pizza, and a German rail gun with a barrel 100 feet long. Joe said he saw Mount Etna erupt, but didn't have the pictures like Elmer.

When Joe came back from the war, he used his military training to get work as a blaster for a company putting in telephone poles. When the crew dug 10-foot-deep holes for large poles, they often hit ledge. Then Joe would come in to drill and blast so they could continue.

Unfortunately, Joe died early at age 52, in 1968, maybe because he was such a heavy smoker.

Elmer, according to his nephew Joe, was an easy-going guy. He entered the army as a private, and left as a private; he wasn't interested in promotions. He was mischievous, and liked to play tricks on others. He was out going, and loved to go to the fire department for the social life. He never married, and that gave him great flexibility. He drove school bus in the winter, then would take off in the summer and do the rodeo circuit out west for a month or more. He also worked as a construction laborer.

As mentioned, Joe's sons Henry and Norman also were in the military. Henry started out in the Army National Guard, then switched to the Air Force which offered more opportunities. Since he was a union bricklayer, young Henry could go off on assignments and easily get a job when he returned. The Union also paid for his medical insurance while he was in Iraq.

Henry said that during his deployment in Iraq, he saw the labs that made the weapons of mass destruction. One was built at the center of a massive parking garage, disguising it from any surveillance. This corroborated a report I (Steve) got from another soldier in Iraq, who said that they had found stockpiles of weapons of mass destruction, but the media had ignored this as it did not fit their preconceptions.

Henry also got to visit some historical sites in Iraq, like the ziggurats, the oldest pyramids in the world.

On one assignment, he was in charge of a repair team working at a remote patrol base. They were repairing a trailer with toilets and showers, when mortars began to fall on the area. They ran for shelter and came away unharmed, but he said it was a scary five minutes.

Henry also went to Israel on a project for the National Guard. Since the food at the army base was not very good, he and his crew ate breakfast in a local truck stop that served bacon. Unfortunately, the Palestinians learned about this and bombed it one morning because Americans were eating there; fortunately, that morning Henry was late for breakfast and wasn't blown up.

Dorothy and Rob Miller

Newt Bingham and Rob Miller were not in the military because they were in occupations important for the war effort-- Newt worked at EB and Robert worked in farming.

Even though they were opposites in temperament, these two were great friends all their lives, often working together on construction jobs. In picture on above, taken at work, Newt is in front, Rob in the upper right. When Newt formed his own company, Rob joined his crew.

They were both extraordinarily strong. Newt looked the part, being barrel-chested and wide shouldered, able to lift boulders alone. Rob, on the other hand, was slight in build, but just as strong, able to do one-handed pull ups. One time at the Brooklyn Fair there was a booth with a device to test grip strength, and Rob did better than Newt! The story is told that Rob once bent a three-quarter inch breaker bar with his bare hands, no pipe used! His daughter, Donna related that, "When my brother was lifting weights with his friends, he challenged my Dad and Dad picked up 225 lbs. as if it were nothing."

Newt married Frances Steward, a girl from Waterford who came to Canterbury to be the teacher of the Westminster school, and later at Gayhead. In the picture above, Rob is the best man, and the bride's maid, Julia Nelson, who later married Henry Miller.

Frances then introduced Rob to her sister, Dorothy, and they married on November 26, 1942 (pictured here on left).

Dorothy Steward was born at home in a blizzard in Waterford, Connecticut on March 2, 1911 and died on January 21, 2015. She was the oldest of five children and grew up doing routine chores on her father's dairy farm.

These included bringing the cows in from the pasture, feeding them, watering and feeding the horses, and bottling and delivering milk. Her favorite task was using the horses to rake hay in the summer. One of her unfulfilled desires was to try harness racing.

Much to her dismay, after her graduation from Chapman Technical High School in New London, her mother enrolled her in the two-year program at the Bay Path Institute. Upon her graduation from Bay Path, she spent a year as the clerk to the Waterford tax assessor. She then got a job teaching home economics at Chapman Technical High School where she taught for ten years.

On her annual salary of $900, she sent her second sister to Willimantic Normal School and two years after that her third sister, Frances (Putty) Steward Bingham to Willimantic Normal School. For the years that both sisters were in school together, Dorothy was left with one hundred dollars to cover all of her expenses.

In spite of this meager income, she was able to have her own car (pictured here). After she and Rob married, she was shocked when he casually let his brother borrow the car that was hers!

After marrying, Dorothy gave up her teaching job to become a full-time homemaker and mother, as she and Rob had five children: Donna (1944), Robert (1946-2015), Paul (1949), Diane (1952) and Royal (1957-1982).

During her child rearing years, she was active in the Grange and in the First Congregational Church of Canterbury. In later years, she was a Deaconess in the church which was a source of great pride to her.

Dorothy considered herself a modern woman. She took full advantage of food technologies, changing from canning garden produce to freezing it when she acquired a freezer. She thought the microwave was a wonderful time saver.

She was a 4-H leader for fifteen years, having established a 4-H group when Donna was old enough to join and then a second group when Diane was of age.

Dorothy enjoyed sewing. She made most of her own clothes as well as those for her children when they were young. She updated her sewing machines as often as possible. In the picture on the left, she wears a dress she made that won an award at the Grange.

She taught sewing to her daughters, granddaughters, nieces, 4-H groups and anyone else who was interested.

She loved fabrics of all kinds and later in life, she began quilting, but she always used a machine to do appliqué, piecing or quilting because she thought it was stronger and more efficient.

She was also a talented needle worker: knitting or crocheting sweaters, embroidering clothing or wall hangings, and tatting trim and ornaments.

Dorothy was a fast, avid reader who always had a book in process. Always interested in the library, she served on the Canterbury Library Board of Trustees.

Her husband, Rob, worked construction intermittently but always was a farmer at heart. As a boy, when he was in the sixth grade, he often stayed home from school, saying he wanted to help his father. Finally, Pop said, "Either go to school, or stay home and work," so Rob quit school after the eighth grade and plunged full time into the occupation he loved.

When his father died in 1939, Rob took over the family farm. In 1953, he and his brother and partner, Elmer, built a state of the art dairy barn on Water Street, complete with glass block windows, and they stocked it with registered Holsteins. During the next ten years, they had two cows which were the top milk producers in New England.

Dairy regulations changed dramatically in the early

60s, so rather than go into debt to build a new pole barn and milking parlor to accommodate them, Rob & Elmer sold the animals and equipment in 1963. Elmer sold his share of the land while Rob rented his to other farmers.

One winter when he was in his late fifties, Rob was standing on a tree limb getting ready to cut with his saw, when the limb broke and he fell backwards, landing in a way that broke his back. He spent the rest of his life, 29 years, in a wheelchair.

Rob told how in his youth, while building the new bridge at Middletown with Newt, he fell off it, landing in the mud 30 feet below. He was able to just get up and walk off. And here he fell only a few of feet and was now incapacitated.

Dorothy was fifty-eight when Rob fell and became a paraplegic. At the time the accident happened, she still had three children living at home and when Rob came home from the hospital, she had to provide all the nursing care needed by a paraplegic, in addition to her normal duties. She continued to care for him at home until his death twenty-nine years later.

With no source of income available, she took a job teaching third grade at St. John's Grammar School in Plainfield. Along with this, she took the tests necessary for becoming a state worker. The following year she was hired as Clerk II at Uncas-on-Thames Hospital where she became a payroll clerk and worked until she retired at age 71.

In her retirement, she was the secretary for the  Commission on Aging and she became C.W.A. chairman.

Dorothy was a registered Republican who voted in every election. She was very interested in politics and had strong opinions about candidates and policies.

Dorothy lived to be 103, and was in good shape nearly to the end, still driving when she was 100. Her sister, Frances

Bingham must have the same genes, as she is 101 at the writing of this book.

Miller Traditions

Beginning in 1958, on the second Sunday of August, the Miller's started a family practice of gathering in their sister's (Dorothea Miller Dean's) shady back yard for a picnic get-together. It was moved, two years later, to brother-in-law Theodore (Ted) Dean's property where everyone gathered around "Cranberry Lake" and enjoyed the raft, canoe, water skis and sailboat along with great food. This tradition continues to today.

This is the story of a hard-working, industrious family, who, by simply making a better life for themselves and their children, became a positive part of Canterbury's history.

Milo Appely 1896-1969
--by Steve

I remember Milo as the milk tester for Windham county. He would come to our farm on Lisbon Road every two or three months and take a sample of the milk every cow produced. These samples were then analyzed to find the percentage of milk fat, which was a determiner of price.

He had his own farm in Canterbury on Route 169 across from Quinnebaug Valley Farm, but had a helper who did the work for him. He sold loose hay by the "Square," a 12

 foot by 12 foot section cut out of the haystack.

As a boy in Canterbury he had his own oxen team; he is the little fellow in this picture, the only one I could find of him.

He served in the Navy in World War I, but I never heard him mention it.

He and his wife, Emma had no children, which maybe is which he was so kind to the children he met. He invited us to fish in his pond and always talked with us when he visited our farm.

Each year he would take the sixth-grade class from Baldwin to Hartford to see the Shriner's circus.

He loved to garden and had big ones; he hired Eleanor Hart, who lived next door, and other children to pick the veggies.

Milo was also president of the Brooklyn Fair Association for many years.

He liked to collect Indian artifacts he found along the river, which included arrowheads and a stone ax.

He enjoyed helping people get loans when they needed it, as he had contacts at the banks and knew how to negotiate.

He's the one who secured a loan to build the first fire house (above) for the newly formed volunteer fire department.

Milo and his wife, Emma, were faithful members of the Grange, where Emma played the piano for events. Milo headed up the project to put in a cellar under the grange building, organizing help to dig it out by hand. The Miller boys and Newt Bingham took many wheelbarrow loads of dirt out from under it!

In the end, Milo came down with cancer. Alton went to visit him in the hospital, and they had such a good, long visit that the nurse had to kick Alton out. Milo died at age 73, while his wife lived to be 100, dying in 1995.

Neil Dupont

--by Sheila

Since 1900 there have been 37 First Selectmen elected to office in Canterbury: George Greene, George Bradford, Fred Richmond, Aaron Moore, Charles Hyde, Marshall Frink, Elmer Bennett, William Barker, Marshall Frink, Levi Clark, E. Fitch Johnson, Edward Baker, Herbert Tracy, Christian Kerr, Arthur Bennett, Theodore Dean, Frederick Willoughby, Curtis Kinne, Fred Cone, George Blood, Theodore Dean, Hans Hansen, Norman Kerr, Robert Laws, Edward Waskiewicz, Andrew Schrader, Lewis Gray, David Ginnetti, Robert Manship, Raymond Guillet, Diane Tripp, Charles Savarese, Sr., Raymond Guillet, Neil Dupont, Sr., Paul Santoro, Neil Dupont, Sr. and Brian Sear. Only one First Selectman has served as First Selectman for ten years–Neil Dupont, Sr.

Neil is used to small town living since he grew up in Voluntown. He moved to Canterbury because of his wife, Adele's, sheep business.

He and a friend went to a wood chopping contest in Lake Dunsmore, Vermont and there he met Adele. They talked on the phone often and he drove up to Vermont to visit her many times. Six months later they were married. "And I'm glad I married her!" Neil said. They had two boys, Neil Jr. and John and today they have three grandchildren: Ryan, Riley and Della.

In 1973 they bought a farm on Barstow Road in Canterbury and moved in on Graff Road with their good neighbors, Randy Hexter, Charles Eastland, Joe Shinnen, and Arthur and Helen LeBeau.

Adele had wanted a place for her own sheep so she could continue to build her business of breeding sheep. She showed her sheep all over the country and when she sold her business in 1989, she had the 3rd best Oxford sheep flock in the United States.

While Adele worked on her business, Neil was a driver for the Cooper Jarett Trucking Company. He drove all over the United States. He also became the company's shop steward. In this position, he learned to be a negotiator between the drivers and management. This gave him experience dealing with people, which would later serve him well when he became First Selectman.

Cooper Jarrett decided to move out of Connecticut to Rhode Island, making it a 50-mile one-way trip for Neil to go to work. Since he already had a small animal feed business, what with the many sheep and other farm animals on his farm, he decided to quit his driving job, and in December of 1979 he opened his own business (Arrowhead Farm Supply) out of a large building on his property.

He said it turned out to be very interesting business because of the people he met through the years. He believed in running the business with a relaxed atmosphere. The door to his grain store was never locked. If he had to leave and run an errand, he left a note telling customers to take what they needed and leave the money on the cash register.

The family didn't take vacations, but they traveled to a lot of sheep shows and fairs. Between shows Adele would keep herself busy making toys from sheepskins. She expanded that business to include her famous slippers and many other items which she makes by hand. Today, Neil and Adele travel the country selling her items. She has been selling her handmade crafts at the Big E since 1978.

Neil is a gun enthusiast and he started skeet and trap shooting when he was 25 years old at the Sprague Rod and Gun Club. Skeet shooting (clay bird) is when two machines shoot two objects in the air across each other and the shooter has shoot both of them for a good score. In trap shooting, the objects are shot away from the shooter in 5 different directions. He loved doing that.

His teacher started taking him to competitions all over New England, New York and New Jersey. Neil says he always was the type of person to put in enough work to win competitions. In 1967 and 1968 he won the Winchester Clay Bird Tournament in Rhode Island. The prize was a pair of specially made Winchester shot guns. One of his proudest moments was in 1968 when he beat his teacher in a competition. He was very happy about that.

Neil joined the Republican Town Committee and in May of 1994 was appointed as a member of the Board of Selectmen with Raymond Guillet and Charles Savarese.

During his second term, he had a heart attack due to a clogged artery. He told me that before the heart attack he would have a dozen eggs and a couple pieces of toast for a snack and 2-3 pounds of bacon while watching television at night. After the attack, he stopped smoking and even today follows a very strict diet. He does cheat sometimes though (don't tell Adele). He says the heart attack has made him appreciate life much more.

In 1995 he thought he could contribute to the betterment of Canterbury so he decided to run for First Selectman and was elected. He knew he could do a good job especially with his experience in business and negotiations with people. He could make decisions and stay cool-headed.

 Also, former Assessor and First Selectman, Charles Savarese, told Neil "I know if you become First Selectmen you will finally get a new town hall built for Canterbury." Neil fulfilled this prediction and, with the Town Hall Building Committee ,saw the completion of the Municipal building in 1995. Above is a picture of the ground-breaking ceremony for the building. Neil is second from the left, the one with the shovel.

241

Neil was First Selectman 1995-2003 and 2005-2007.

Here's Neil with his favorite secretary, Sheila Mason Gale.

Other than the new town municipal building, he had a number of other accomplishments while in office. When he took office, the newest truck in the Public Works fleet was 20 years old, so he increased the Capital Improvement Plan to replace trucks and buses more often.

Raymond Guillet initiated the transfer station idea and Neil continued this, developing it into a working transfer station. He added more money to the budget and improved the Canterbury road system.

Having been a shop steward, he realized Canterbury employees were underpaid and began a program to get their wages up with other towns.

He moved the War Memorial from the school to municipal building and the War Memorial Committee expanded it.

In June of 2003, Neil and about 12 dedicated citizens organized, in only three weeks, a 4th of July parade/town activity and made the event a success. That year a profit of about $8,000 was made and donated to the War Memorial.

He supported emergency generators in the school and municipal building, so if an emergency arose in Canterbury, we would be able to meet citizen's needs. He was a member of the Fire Department and he also served Canterbury by becoming an EMT and going on ambulance calls. In 2001 he was the top responder.

As with any First Selectman, there could be controversy, but he could separate personal feelings from politics. Neil was known for "telling it like it is". He enjoyed being First Selectman because he liked talking with all kinds of people and listening to people's stories, thoughts and ideas.

Neil thinks the biggest change in town since moving to Canterbury in the 1970's is that some people are moving in to town from larger cities and they want to change Canterbury to be like a big town. "When you do that, you lose the closeness of the people in town. We need to keep that small-town closeness in our community".

Newt 1920-1994 **and Frances Bingham** 1916
--by Steve

Newt came from a long line of Binghams in Connecticut. Thomas Bingham was born in Yorkshire England in 1642. He arrived in Saybrook Connecticut with his mother in 1659, at the age of 17. His father probably died on  the way over. They moved to Norwich when his mother married William Backus Sr.

In 1815 Uriah Bingham bought land in Canterbury and farmed there, as did his descendants, including Newt's father, Byron. In the picture above are the students at Gayhead School with Byron being the short fellow in the back row, showing the stocky, strong build of the Binghams. In the picture below, Byron holds a horse with his children Dotty, Tom, Newt and Alice sitting on it.

 Like most farmers of his time, he had milk cows, and took his full milk cans to Scotland to be put on the train to Rhode Island. He supplemented his milk income with cutting chestnut trees for railroad ties. Byron died quite early from a back injury, probably sustained in his wood cutting work.

Newt went to Sunday School with the Miller boys, first to the Scotland church and then to Westminster. He was serious about his beliefs and made a commitment to Christ before becoming a teen. This new relationship with Christ set the tone for the rest of his life, as evidenced by his integrity, graciousness and clean living.

At 16 Newt left high school in his sophomore year after his father died and went to work to support the family. His first job was with the town road crew. He ended up being the crew chief.

Art freeman, one of the workers, told the story of them pulling a conveyor to a gravel bank, chaining it to the back of the town truck, which was a new Studebaker. Two of the crew members wanted to ride on the conveyor, but Newt wouldn't let them, which turned out to be a good thing. On the way down Bennet Pond Road, the conveyor came loose and careened off the road and turned over.

Art said that Newt, in his no-nonsense way, didn't make a big thing out it. He got his men to tip it back up, clean up the motor and hitch it again to the truck.

Alex Risavich said Newt gave him a job on the town crew when Alex was sixteen and they spent a lot of time cutting brush along the roads. Alex remembers a time when they were trying to move a large rock by hand, but were unable to budge it. Right then Newt came up to see how they were doing, asked them to step back from the rock and moved it effortlessly out the way single handedly. Alex also said that Newt was a fine person, never swearing, never getting angry, always treated his men well.

In those days, it was common for the boys to do some boxing after work. Newt went further and decided to try his hand at some more advanced fighting, going to New Haven for a match or two. A number of his Canterbury friends came along to cheer him on. He was outmatched, but refused to go down and made the other boxer earn his victory. He lost on points, not a knock out.

 In 1938 Newt married Francis Steward, whom he met at the Grange. She was a teacher in the one room school houses in Canterbury, first in Westminster, then in Gayhead. Alex Risavich, who attended the Gayhead school for several years, commented on what a kind person Mrs. Bingham was. She noticed that he had a cold sore that bothered him and the next

day brought some ointment that gave him relief and then healing. The picture below is of Frances' class at

Westminster School; she is right in the middle of the back row with the shine over her head.

Frances was a committed, born again follower of Jesus, having come to faith slowly over her childhood, attending church and reading the Bible on her own. She continued to grow in her faith throughout her life, and when I spoke to her today, at 101 she is still positive, interested in talking about her faith, and looking forward to going to heaven when she dies.

She told me about her arrival in Canterbury and how God orchestrated things for her. Malcolm Wibberley was the chairman of the school board and had hired her to teach at the Westminster School. So, when she moved to Canterbury, she went first to his farm to find out where she might stay. He referred her to Mrs. Hawes who lived at the Green, where another teacher, Julia, was boarding. Frances went to the Green and Mrs. Hawes, after asking Julia's permission, agreed to have Frances board there, too.

Frances told me, "This was clearly the Lord's help and provision for me, as Julia had a car and drove right by the Westminster School house on her way to Gayhead, so she could give me a ride!"

In this picture, taken in 1943, Newt and Frances pose in front of their house.

Newt eventually left the town road crew position for a job in construction. He worked building the present Butts Bridge as well as the new bridge over the Connecticut River at Middle Town.

The boss for that job miscalculated while removing the old steel bridge and it fell into the river. They couldn't leave it there because it would impede river traffic, so Newt was put in charge of dealing with the situation. The bridge was far too heavy to be lifted out with the cranes they had, but Newt found that he could use the current of the river, along with a crane, to roll the submerged bridge over and over towards a sand bar. Then, as a part of the bridge rolled up onto the bar he would have that cut off, then roll it again so more was exposed to be cut. His Yankee ingenuity saved the day for his boss.

In this picture taken at work, Newt is sitting on the

lower step on the left. Behind him on the right is Rob Miller.

As mentioned, Newt was exceptionally strong and his fellow workers figured out a way to capitalize on that. On the way home from a hot day's work, they'd stop at a bar and bet the other patrons a case of beer that Newt could do a one-handed pull up. A broom was produced and held up by two strong men; Newt easily did his one-handed chin-up and the crew got a case of beer. Newt, being a nondrinker, just took a soda.

Rob Miller was Newt's good friend, and was also very strong, able to do one handed pull ups, too. He once bent a Snap-on Tool pry bar with his bare hands. He took over a farm on Water Street, which was covered with poison ivy, but the cows ate it all. He worked for Newt and farmed part time.

Newt and Frances had three children, Mary, Newt Jr. and Janice. In the picture on the right, Newt holds his little son, Newt Jr.

Both Newt and Frances were strong committed Christians, faithful attenders of Westminster Church. In fact, Newt's strong commitment to Christ was the major factor in Frances marrying him. He had been a regular attender of Sunday School as a child, going with the Miller boys.

Newt, with one of his fellow workers, formed a construction business of their own, Bingham and Chilkott, and they specialized in building smaller bridges. In his later years Newt's company built the bridge on Route 14 over Kitt Brook.

Newt died in 1964 at the age of 77. Frances, being from a long-lived family, as of the writing of this book in 2017 is 101 and going strong, cared for my her daughter, Janice.

In this picture are three generations of John Newton Binghams. Newt Jr. lives in Alaska and worked for many years for the Alaskan Highway system.

Papuga Family
--by Sheila

In 1950 Walter and Mary Papuga sold a store they owned in

Massachusetts, bought a house at the north end of Water Street and moved to Canterbury with their two sons Danny and David.

The front of their house was a small convenience shop known as the Westminster Hill store. They sold canned goods, groceries, cold cuts, hamburger meat, ice cream, and other basics, along with newspapers. It is much like the local store that is in the

center of the Town of Scotland today. Mary and Walter ran the store during the day and Walter worked at Brand Rex in Willimantic at night. In the picture to the left, Walter and Mary do a little Polka outside their store.

The store had its regular local customers. As a boy, Raymond Coombs, Sr. remembers Mary as always looking out for the kids in the neighborhood. She would tell them to button their coats and put the flaps down on their hats in the winter. Actually, she would look out for everybody.

The LaBranche family, on Brooklyn Road, came in every weekend to get Sunday night supper. Noreen LaBranche Kjos remembers her Dad buying salami and bologna, chips and ice cream. Noreen says going to the store on Sunday was a family outing. Unlike today there were no local pizza shops in the area that families could go to. Steve

249

Wibberley remembers going every Sunday after church to get a newspaper.

Noreen also remembers when she worked for Lew Gray at Verkades Nursery, Mildred "Ma" Coombs would let the workers walk to the Papuga store for a treat. Mary Papuga would put popsicle sticks in candy bars and freeze them for cool treats. One summer Mary's two sisters Olive and Foo Foo had an ice cream stand next to the store.

I remember riding horses all around town with Judy Simpson and we would often stop at the store, tie our horses up out front and go in for ice cream.

Mary became a widow at an early age when Walter died at 42, but she continued running the store until her sons were out of high school. When the store closed, Cliff Green, Sr. helped her get a job at UConn.

Mary would go with Eleanor Orlomoski to the Bingo hall located where Foxwoods Casino is today. Eleanor said Mary's mind was so sharp she didn't have to use markers on her Bingo cards, she simply remembered all the numbers called.

Frances Vaclavik delivered the Papuga's mail and said Mary was a cheerful, happy lady. Good fortune came Mary's way when she won the Connecticut state lottery.

Growing up in Canterbury, Danny remembers his teachers Mrs. Elva Lovell and Mrs. Happie K. Tracy. They were tough, but good teachers, he said. As he looks back on it now, he gives them both a lot of credit because they did not have any helpers. It was only one teacher and all the students.

Danny Papuga started working for Tom Bingham in construction at $3.00 per hour. He eventually worked his way up to being a foreman. His brother David went on to get a degree in civil engineering.

Danny thought he should stop making money for someone else, so he and his brother started the Papuga Construction Company and did a lot of State work, such as bridges, and construction at the Plainfield dog track. They also volunteered to help maintain the Canterbury athletic fields.

Today David lives in Putnam and Danny still lives in Canterbury. He retired 5 years ago and now he likes to go golfing and play with his grandchildren, Isabel, Ayden and Harrison.

Danny says his mother Mary had a heart of gold. He was glad Mary and Walter raised him in Canterbury and says it is still a beautiful place to raise children. That's what draws families here. Canterbury is simply a nice place to live.

Paula Fontaine 1903-1982
--by Steve

Paula Meinhole was born in 1904 in Germany in the village of Wiesendorf, shown in the painting below.

In 1907 her parents emigrated to America, entering through Ellis Island. They first lived with relatives in New Jersey, but soon bought a large tract of land in Canterbury around the intersection of Lisbon and Gooseneck Hill Roads.

The 218 acres of land included Bates Pond and they would allow people to come in to the pond during the winter to cut ice so they could store it for use in the summer. In the picture below, from right to left, are Paula, her brother, Ed, her

father, Oswold Meinhold, and her other brother, Oswin.

When Lisbon Road was redone and paved in the 1940s, the inspector in charge of the project, Frank Ginnetti, bought the Bates Pond portion of their land.

Paula married a Mr. Freeman and had two sons, Art and Clarence, but the marriage didn't last long. Several years later she married Jerry Fontaine, a Navy man who had lost a leg in the service, and had three more children with him, Jerry, Charlotte and Fred. This marriage also did not last that long.

252

Perhaps because of all the difficulties she suffered in life, Paula sought strength in the spiritual realm. She was invited to go to a meeting in Norwich where the speaker was a Jewish man who had come to know Jesus as his Messiah and Savior. Paula responded to his message, accepted Christ as her Savior and was born again. She became a faithful attender at Calvary Chapel and brought with her all her children still at home.

Paula's house in the early years, was, like most others at the time, reasonably primitive. There was a hand pump in the kitchen with a pipe running to the sink. In the winter, Paula would put a kerosene lantern next to the pipe to keep it from freezing. But she was not content to stay there. She got electricity and running water long before many others. The picture of her house below was probably taken in the early 40s.

Paula had two sides to her personality. She was a tough and determined person who didn't let anyone push her around. She had poppies growing in her flower garden and the police  came to tell her this was illegal, but she told them it was none of their business and to leave. And they did!

When CL&P wanted to cut down a tree on the edge of her property, she strongly objected. CL&P called the police, and when the police realized this call was about Paula Fontaine, they told CL&P to not bother her!

She planted flowers along the edge of the road, and  when the town crew came along to cut the brush, they also cut the flowers. Well, as seen in the picture on the left, they got an earful from Paula about that!

On the other hand, Paula loved people, regularly visiting shut-ins and neighbors. Wherever she went, she would interact with people, showing genuine interest and concern.

She also loved gardening, especially flowers. And she loved to share her flowers with others. Her daughter, Charlotte, told of going often to visit old people who couldn't get out, and all summer long Paula would bring them flowers.

Paula never had a regular job, and, as most of the time she had no husband who provided for her, she had to find ways to feed her family. She raised chickens, sold the eggs,  had cows and sold milk and butter, had a big vegetable garden and sold some of that. She raised strawberries and would pick wild blue berries to sell. In the picture on the left , taken in 1947 is her barn and milk house. After her children left home, Paula supported herself by cleaning for other people.

Although she had gone through difficult times and experienced a lot of hurt, Paula tended to trust people and think the best of them. One neighbor family with seven children had a hard time because the husband was a drinker, so Paula often visited them and brought them vegetables, milk, eggs and flowers. She found a baker who would sell her a bag of older bread for 25 cents each week and she would take it to this family.

Paula was big on canning, doing corn, beans, peas, blueberries and strawberries and other foods. One time when she was set to can her beans, she went out to the garden to pick them and found that all her beans were gone! Every plant was picked clean. Well that made her mad!

Later that day she went to visit that poor family, and there saw a big tub full of fresh beans in the kitchen. This family didn't

have a garden, so she asked where they came from. The wife said her husband had brought them home. Paula knew exactly where they came from, but because of her love for the wife, never said a word.

Later when this family moved away to Vermont, Paula went up and visited them.

When her three youngest were quite small, a woman relative of hers was killed in an accident, so Paula took in her three boys and cared for them for several years, even though their father never sent her any money.

Both Charlotte (in the picture below with her daughter  and Paula) and Art said that Paula was a wonderful mother, and part of that was her not letting them get away with anything. A curse word brought on a mouthful of soap or castor oil. Work had to be done right and completely. Her grand daughters, Darlene and Cindy, told how they were given the task of ironing handkerchiefs but they got tired of it and left before finishing. Paula brought them right back and made sure they completed the job!

Paula had some special talents. She was very adept at finding four leaf clovers—which she kept pressed in a book--and could catch a fly in the air. She also had some special beliefs, like drinking castor oil to keep her creaking knees lubricated.

She was able to live at home until the very end, only spending one day in the hospital before she died. She left her family and neighbors a legacy of hard work, practicality, grace and love—a real Canterbury character.

Philip J. Cleveland 1903-1995
--by Steve

In the span of his life's ministry, Reverend Philip Cleveland served several existing churches and reopened four closed churches, including the one that the famous missionary, David Brainerd (1718-17470), had originally organized.

Before coming to Canterbury, Mr. Cleveland was pastor of the Brooklyn Congregational Church, but when it was so badly damaged in the Hurricane of 1938, he was transferred to the Westminster Church and served there from 1942 to 1958.

When he came to Westminster, there were only 5 active members, and his pay was $5 each Sunday.

Pictured here on the left with his wife, he was a warm, people-loving person, very interested in helping those he served. That showed in the growth of his congregation, as by 1944 there were 45 active members.

He was ready to help anyone who came along: to come alongside the Indian who needed a lawyer; to search most of the night for two teen age girls who had run away from an orphanage on a cold November night to escape a child molester (Pastor Cleveland did find and protect them); to visit unfriendly and shunned folks, helping them out of their loneliness; to visit a parishioner every afternoon in Willimantic, as she was dying of cancer, and help her find peace.

He was also a hard worker, clearing woodlots for farmers to get free firewood--he was a man who knew how to get things done.

And he was an artist with paints and the piano, often playing duets with Frances Bingham. He was also an artist with words, writing several books. One is called, *Three Churches and a Model T,* which tells a lot about his ministry in Canterbury. It is a book worth reading, available in the

256

Canterbury Library, and you can find it online.

Below I'll quote edited portions of two chapters of his book to give you a taste of his talent, as well as some insight into his ministry in Canterbury.

The Church without a voice.[4]

"Is the minister in?" a short stocky man said to my wife on the sun-shot back steps to the manse one propitious Monday morning.

When I opened the door, he smiled, a blue cap in hand, work overalls a fire in the molten sunglow. His whole attitude was one of force full business. "Say, preacher, do you really want that bell hung? You said yesterday that the church had no voice. Perhaps get that old church talking again. I'm a truck driver. We have two weeks' vacation on hand and I think I can do it!"

The day before I had informed the Canterbury folks that we should rebuild the belfry smashed by the 1938 hurricane. Here

it was, 1946, and the seven hundred/ pound bell still sat silent inside the large green church doors.

[Editor's note: I could not find a picture of the damaged Westminster Church, but this picture of one in R.I. which lost its steeple, will give you a sense of the destructive power of the hurricane]

The 175th anniversary of Westminster church was coming up in a few weeks. Why not ring out the old, ring in the new?

Collecting the senior deacon, Fredrick A. Hicks, the three of us went to a saw mill deep in the tangled woodlands of Plainfield. Said Hans to the owner "I got to have three one-thousand-pound oak timbers."

---

[4] Quotes from the rest of this chapter taken from *Three Churches and a Model T,* Phillip Jerome Cleveland, Revell, a division of Baker Publishing Group, Copyright 1960, used with permission.

"Ain't got 'em," was the brisk retort.

"You can get them," challenged Hans.

The next day, at dusk, three oak timbers and an assorted pile of lumber were stacked in the church yard and the following morning Hans led his gang into the hurricane-smashed building. One youth was Russian, another Norwegian, another French, another Finnish, and still another a German.

Hans was here, there and everywhere, directing, ordering, correcting, readjusting, superintending as the men slowly lifted a belfry towards the blue skies.

I asked him about the blueprints.

"Blueprints?" he bellowed leaning back in the chair. From a dirty shirt pocket, he drew forth a small scrap of paper with a dozen pencil marks across it. "That's all the blueprint I have up to now. More will come later after I dream over the problems. More always comes."

The carriage, the rocker of the bell, had been smashed by the hurricane. Hans wrestled with how to replace it. One morning he said "Let's go to the junkyard. I got me an idea." Two hours later he returned with an iron skeleton tied to his car.

Hans struggled with another man to lift the queer auto part, the skeleton thing upstairs and soon the seven hundred/pound bell was making incredible music high atop

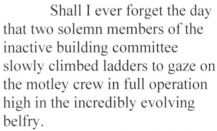

Westminster hill.

Shall I ever forget the day that two solemn members of the inactive building committee slowly climbed ladders to gaze on the motley crew in full operation high in the incredibly evolving belfry.

"Reverend, how is it that these men are here?"

"I invited them."

"On what authority?"

As the bell rang, I quoted a famous passage from David Lloyd George, the embattled British premier: "The

258

finest eloquence is that which gets things done; the worst is that which delays them."

In the picture above, taken in the 1950s, is the steeple Hans and his men built for Westminster Church.

A Sermon for the Family

I sat down Saturday morning to meditate on Sunday's message, already completed, a message on hope and vision, when that sermon went as flat as yesterday's pancake. Suddenly I realized that there wasn't anything in it for the people.

Scanning the typed pages, an invisible wind stirred through the study: "You ought to preach a sermon on the Christian home. It has been considerable time since you delivered a message on Christ in the home."

The idea of children seized me with a strange, challenging impact. How little children need the love and tender care of Christian parents! Do children have a fair chance in life who do not sense the charm, the beauty of Christ in their parents, in the devotions of the home, in the everyday experiences of daily life?

This thought came to me out of somewhere, blowing into the inner laboratories, stirring the hidden vitalities. That entire sermon came to me like Peter's sheet let down from an unexpected height.

I was amazed at the last-minute Sunday message, "Christ in the Home," at its apparent logic, freshness, and challenge.

I knew it would be the next day's offering and it was. Not until I was ready to stand and deliver it did I observe a strange family moving up the east aisle, slipping into a side pew. Four of these six latecomers were small children, three girls, one boy.

It was not long before I became aware of the intense interest of the lady. She had slumped in the pew; she was now becoming alert, her body stiffening, straightening. The eyes grew brighter, the face moved forward in expectancy.

This lady could not have been more than thirty-five. She stood out among a hundred communicants as a detached point of vision, a shining target for the gospel marksman. She made herself the perfect target, her eyes riveted upon the altar, her full, round face, rapt, wistful.

As I preached, noticing the three girls, the boy, I became convinced that this sermon had been specifically designed for them.

Following the benediction, the family lingered on the lawn at the edge of the church entrance. When I stepped from the porch to the ground, the lady was at my side, four children clinging to her, a lean, quiet man just behind. She had been waiting outside some twenty minutes as two deacons inside mentioned matters of urgent business.

"I want to thank you, pastor, for that message. It was exactly what I needed, what we all need, especially the little ones!" Her arms were flung about four wiggling, gaily colored forms swaying about the orchid dress. "It was exactly what I needed, what Al needs, what we all need especially the little ones."

"Wasn't that a sermon, Al?" she said turning back to her husband. who grinned and nodded.

"Would it be asking too much, pastor, to call on us this week? It is quite urgent. Do you think you could call soon? I do not wish to appear dramatic, but it would mean a great deal to have you call." She lowered her musical voice to the merest whisper. "I really need help, can you come?"

"I will be over this week without fail," I assured her. I watched six strangers, a little family that had filled a pew, now moving towards a parked car.

Thursday afternoon I followed directions to a handsome new house in a housing development and was ushered into the house by the lady, who immediately launched into her story.

"I must tell you about everything pastor, I thought you might have to face a crisis when you called this week. But you don't!"

"Would you mind letting me in on the secret?" I suggested.

"Well, pastor, I took out my first divorce papers. I left him once before. This time I was determined to separate from him for good.'

"You both began to be interested in others?" I asked.

"No pastor, nothing like that. I just began to dislike Al, to hold him off, to build a wall between us.

"A man I ride to work with who attends your church, found out my plans and asked me if I had given God a chance. He said I ought to go to church once before making further plans. His words bothered me, and so we came on Sunday."

Returning home after the service, she had become unusually aware of the children, she said. Had she realized before what the children meant to her and what she must mean to them?

"Something happened to me between your church and my house" she declared. "I am going to learn to be a first-class wife and mother. I owe that to Al and the children. See what I have put over the fireplace in the next room," and she led the way, pointing to the plaque there.

"Christ is the head of this house,
The unseen guest at every meal,
The silent listener to every conversation."

"Oh, it's so wonderful!" she triumphed. "Through the church, we have found our home, our children, our love again!"

She and her husband became regular attenders, raising their children well, and today are leaders in my son's Connecticut church, all because the Lord led me to ditch my sermon and take His!

[Editor's note: I hope you enjoyed this glimpse into the remarkable life of Pastor Cleveland, and again, I encourage you to borrow a copy of his book, *Three Churches and a Model T,* from the Canterbury Library.]

Rene and Valerie Beauchene

--by Steve

Rene's family has been in Canterbury for just a century. In 1918 Rene's grandfather, Adelard, and his brother, Bill bought 210 acres on Brooklyn Road and split the land between them. Rene's father, Clarence, who was born on the farm in 1920, had a sister, Dorothy, and a brother, Ernie.

Clarence (in picture on left) served in WW II as a tail gunner on a bomber flying out of England. He was reluctant to talk much about it but he did say that when the shields were rolled back from his gunner's bubble after leaving England, he was exposed to 40 below zero temperatures with the wind blowing in and that he got frost bite more than once. He said he had to focus on the enemy planes in his range and never knew how many he shot down.

After surviving flying twenty-five missions over Germany, he was going to be sent to the Pacific to be a tail gunner there, but was able to become an instructor for tail gunners and was saved from further combat.

Rene was born in 1947 in Willimantic, the oldest of three raised on the little farm his father had. Rene's brother Michael was 4 years younger, and Cindy was 8 years his junior.

Rene said he was quite a rascal, meeting frequently

with his mother's paddle. For example, when his brother Michael was a baby in a playpen outside, Rene 'borrowed' his father's handsaw and cut enough upright bars to free his brother from his prison so they could play together. In this picture, Rene is getting ready to kick his little brother! When he was about seven, Rene tried to escape from the paddle his mother used by breaking it, but she just got a bigger one. He never touched that one.

 I (Steve) first met Rene (pronounced by everyone as "Rainy") while in Baldwin grade school, as he was one grade behind  us. I remember him as a small but solid fellow. After Baldwin, Rene went to Griswold, graduating in 1965. At that time, everyone not going to college was being drafted for the war, so Rene decided to join the Navy to avoid going to Viet Nam.

In the Navy he was assigned to the Seabees, which is like the  army engineers. He was also trained as a machine gunner in basic training (picture on left), and he did some firing of mortars.

After he sent off one mortar round in training, a Marine sergeant came running up to the group and shouted, "Who shot that mortar?" When Rene confessed it was him, the sergeant said, "I want you in my Marine unit! You hit the target exactly!" Rene, however was not interested.

In Vietnam the Seabees were stationed next to the Marines' camp where there were big eight inch guns that went off all night. When a truce came, the guns stopped; Rene said the silence was unnerving and he had trouble sleeping without the noise.

He worked in construction, building and rebuilding water towers, housing and bridges, but also had to stand guard duty at times as in the picture here.

While working on one water tower, Rene was 30 feet off the ground, standing on a 2x4 while hanging onto another as he worked with a big drill; suddenly the 2x4 he was standing on came loose and left him hanging. He was thankful that the second 2x4 held. So are we!

His second tour in Vietnam was easier, working on buildings on a big base in DeNang where there was little interaction with the enemy.

After returning to the States, Rene was sent to Guantanamo Bay in Cuba for about a year, which, he said, was like being in a prison. He related that every day Cubans would sneak onto the base, risking their lives to get on one of the flights leaving from there for South America.

He got out of the Navy in September of 1969 and came back to Canterbury where he worked on construction for a year, and then went to trade school, studying to be an electrician.

In October of 1970, Rene got reacquainted with Valerie Champany, who'd been one year ahead of him in school. Valerie's parents and their ten children (she was number seven) moved to Canterbury when Valerie was in 7th grade. In our class picture from that year (below), Valerie is in white in the middle of the second row from the front.

She was a serious girl and as a small child had been searching for God as a good Catholic.

After finishing Baldwin, she went to Griswold for two years, then transferred to Ellis Tech where she studied hairdressing. But she decided this wasn't for her and returned to Griswold where she graduated from high school. She then worked in several banks as an auditor and bookkeeper for the next seven years.

Valerie related how she was miserable as a teenager. She was a good

264

student, had a good job, and lots of friends, but was very depressed, having many physical problems. Her mother had had the measles during the first trimester of her pregnancy with Valerie, which resulted in Valerie having a number of serious internal birth defects.

She often said to herself, "There's got to be more to life than this!" and related that the only reason she didn't commit suicide was that the Catholic Church taught it was a mortal sin which would send her to hell. She went into a convent four times, hoping to draw closer to God to fill the void in her life, but only became more depressed. During this difficult time her real support system was her mother who was very loving and kind.

She began dating Rene in late 1970, which gave her a new direction in life that looked hopeful.

During his trade school training, Rene began to work part time for Max Wibberley in his tire shop. When Rene finished his schooling, Max told him he would pay him whatever he'd make as an electrician if he'd stay, and Rene ended up working there for nine years.

For many of those years, I (Steve) ran the shop and really was glad to have Rene there. He was an energetic, smart and creative worker. Often in the afternoon, I'd run out of energy and could ride on Rene's boundless energy for the rest of the day.

Rene was not only good at the hard labor of changing tires, he was also a good mechanic and served as our front-end man when we put in an alignment machine.

Rene was still a rascal and liked to play jokes on people. When my father played his trumpet, our dog would often howl along with him. So, one day when Dad was playing, Rene and Ricky Miller went down by his house and howled with the dog. Dad just came out and chased them away.

Rene also enjoyed giving me a hard time about my faith, something I spoke about often and tried to live out in the context of the shop. He never missed an opportunity to kid or ridicule me, and would sometimes try to hamper me as I was talking to a customer about spiritual issues. I would often come home to my wife, bemoaning the difficulty of dealing with Rene, while at the same time being very glad for his contributions to the shop.

Rene and Val married in 1971 and Valerie got  pregnant on their honeymoon. However, she had multiple hospitalizations during tis pregnancy, and then lost the baby, a little boy, at 18 weeks. Because she was weak, they couldn't do a cesarean, so she went through 72 hours of labor, and in the end lost so much blood that she clinically died, flat lined. This seemingly horrible experience changed her for the rest of her life.

She said while she was dead, she was outside of her body, looking down on herself lying on the table with the doctor and nurses around her. She was aware of a light shining on her from behind and watched the doctor pull off his mask and say sadly, "We lost her!"

Just then another doctor came in and said, "We aren't going to give up!" Valerie said that at that point she seemed to have a choice to go or stay and decided to stay. The second doctor then put the paddles on her two times and then the next thing she knew was waking up in the hospital.

That whole "near death" experience made her very aware of God's presence, and it was at this point that she gave her life to the Lord, choosing to trust Him and gaining a new reality of God in her life, beginning to set her free from her misery and fear.

Valerie continued to have 6 more miscarriages between 1971 and 1974. and then had a hysterectomy. They hoped that would be the end of her medical problems.

She continued to struggle spiritually, even though she had a very good knowledge of the Bible. After being born again following her near death experience, she tried to stay in the Catholic Church, but struggled to make that work. She was bothered by what she understood the Church taught about miscarried children.

She went to her priest and asked tearfully, "Are all my seven, miscarried, dead children, who were never baptized, never going to see God?" The priest had difficulty answering with what he taught to be the truth, but finally said, "Yes, they are all in limbo." That was the last straw and Valerie decided to leave the Church.

In 1975, the one ovary she had left ruptured. Not knowing how serious her condition was, she drove herself to a lab in Norwich Town for tests, but felt so bad that she went into Friendly's first to get something to eat. There she collapsed and almost died again, but God was looking after her.

A lineman who was at the register was trained in CPR and immediately went to work on her, continuing his work on the ambulance ride to the hospital, and saving her life. She was unconscious for two days but recovered. This was followed by three more surgeries on ovarian parts, as large tumors reoccurred over the next few years.

When the tumor returned for a fourth time, Valerie heard of a priest who had healing services. So, she asked Rene to take her to see him; the priest prayed over her and she was healed—completely healed! This was confirmed when her surgeon examined her and was amazed to find that the tumor was gone!

This event was so earth shaking that Rene, the skeptical, mocking, anti-religious Rene, bowed his knee to God and accepted Christ as his Savior. Rene and Val prayed together at home, using the prayer from the back of a "chic tract," pictured here below

Rene commented, "The fact that the Lord would let my wife be sick for thirty years just to get my attention so I would surrender to him blows my mind!" God, of course, had more reasons than this for Valerie's illnesses, but knew what needed to be done to get Rene's attention.

God continued to work greatly in and through and for Rene and Val. With all their medical problems, they ended up owing more than $100,000 to doctors and hospitals. For the 1970s this was a huge amount—and their insurance refused to pay. John Wasko suggested they apply to the Army Navy Relief fund, and their whole bill was taken care of!

Rene had left the tire shop in 1979 to start his own business, calling it Beauchene and Sons, even though at the time he had only one adopted son. He briefly did foundations, then switched to general construction.

Right after Val was healed and Rene accepted Christ, the Lord provided him a job on Cape Cod that was supposed to  be for three months, but ended up being seven months. This took Rene away from the negative influence of his drinking buddies in Canterbury and gave them a chance to get established in a good church with new friends who were supportive of their young faith.

Val said It was a wonderful experience for them as a family. At that time, they had two boys they had adopted in 1977 and 1980. Later they adopted a "sibling group" of three in 1984 and, finally, another child in 1987. Four of them were special-needs children. Val homeschooled all of them but one. All six are in the picture on the previous page

When they moved back to Canterbury from the Cape in 1981, Rene picked up his own construction business and they found a good church in Norwich.

After that church moved to MA, they began a church in their home with people they had led to a living relationship with Christ. They called it "the Upper Room," as they met in the room above their garage. So, in the end, the Lord moved Rene from being my (Steve's) persecutor to being the pastor of many! Only God could do that.

As time went on, they rented a place in Central Village and called the church "Tabernacles of Grace," referring to the fact that the Holy Spirit lives in each believer, making them a dwelling place of grace.

Rene and Valerie are co-pastors, sharing in preaching and leadership. Sometimes their son, Robby, also their youth-pastor, preaches and speaks at the men's' breakfasts. His wife, Jackie, conducts the women's meetings. Two of Rob and Jackie's seven children are musicians in the worship team.

Over the years, Rene hasn't made a lot of money with his construction business, not by any means, but has always had enough to live on and to share with others. They have a lot of company, especially on Sunday afternoons and, by the grace of God, have been able to feed them all. Val said It's almost like Jesus feeding the 5, 000, as they have so much company to feed, but always have enough.

Along with raising 6 children and homeschooling five of them, while helping to lead a church, Val has earned her doctorate in theology from Colorado Theological Seminary. She is also an international speaker at conferences, traveling to Cuba, Mexico, and Africa.

In addition, she has written 42 books. Some are teaching (theological) books, some are children's books. One is on the biblical approach to overcoming sexual abuse called *The Paralysis of Unforgiveness*, based on her own testimony. She has a series called *Every Kid Should Be Someone's Hero*. Others are historical novels in a series called *If I Had Been There*, books that place the main character, a teenager, in a situation in the past to help them experience what it was like to live then.

Val says that after her healing and seeing Rene come to Christ, the most significant happening was seeing her mother and father come to Christ, her father accepting Christ on his death bed and visibly changing.

So Rene and Val, now in their 70s, soldier on for Jesus, serving Him and others, bringing life, love and joy to those around them.

No one, looking at their early lives, would ever have predicted such a wonderful outcome, but our God is the great "untwister" of negatives, transforming them into gracious and powerful positives.

Rick Green 1955-1997
--by Steve

Rick was raised here in Canterbury and worked as a carpenter, specializing in installing vinyl siding and windows, having his own business part of the time. Early on he developed genetic diabetes, a disease each member of his family had in spite of their all be in shape and active, and he died at age 42.

His life was short but it turned out well. After some bumpy times early on in his life, after he got sick he returned to the faith of his childhood and began to live out what he had early espoused.

In his youth he had intellectually believed all the Bible taught and had prayed to accept Christ as his Savior, but had, like me, not really surrendered to God but went on to run his own life. However after truly surrendering to Christ as a result of his sickness, Rick's life took on a shininess in the midst of tragedy that put us all to shame.

Here's an entry about Rick from my book *EDIFIED! 365 Devotionals*

"Take up the shield of faith with which you can quench all the fiery darts of the wicked one."

Ephesians 6:14

The fiery darts, the negatives of life, may come *from* the hand of the devil, but come *with* the permission of God and God intends to use them to drive us into the Bible for help and into the arms of Jesus for strength.

We get to choose whether to take His hand and cooperate with the Lord, or to let the our natural self lead us into the swamp of self-pity, anger and despair.

Recently I visited Rick Green, a fellow I've known from his youth, now 40 years old. Humanly speaking he is in bad shape, and has been for years. Having severe genetic diabetes (even though he is not at all overweight), he has had parts of both legs amputated, first below the knees, then above them, as well as some fingers; his kidneys have failed so he is on dialysis 3 times a week; his arms are one mass of scars from infections from plastic inserts to deal with dialysis; he has continual reflux and scaring on his esophagus, partly from severe vomiting when he was poisoned by infections in his legs; in addition, he has experienced heart attacks and insulin attacks and could die at any time.

My intent in visiting him was to give him some encouragement and perspective. How wrong I was! I'm the one who came away encouraged!

Sitting there in his wheelchair, Rick was cheerful, upbeat and positive. He said that he is still alive because God has a purpose for his life. He believes that his job is to pray, so he intercedes about everything: what he sees on the news, what he hears from others, the people he has met in his medical world.

He may be handicapped humanly speaking, but he is focused spiritually on what God has for him. He has allowed these difficulties to drive him into the arms of Jesus, not into the swamp of despair and bitterness. I'm sure that he has had his times of discouragement and self-pity, but he has moved out of them into the light of God's continual presence.

I thought to myself, "If I were in Rick's place, would I think positively like that?" The answer is, humanly speaking, "No!" But if, like Rick, any one of us took up the grace of God and let these difficulties drive us into the Bible for comfort and perspective, and into a deeper dependence on God, we, too, could be joyfully useful in His hand.

Hebrews 12:15 says, "Take heed lest any man fail of the grace of God [meaning we fail to take up and use the grace that God offers], lest any root of bitterness springing up trouble you and many thereby be defiled." Rick is a living example of obeying this verse and principle.

He takes up the grace of God every day and rejects the temptation of self-pity and selfish thinking, instead praising God in and for all. Therefore, he is not bitter, and does not spread the poison of discontent to others; instead he is sweet, bringing help and joy to all he meets. May we who have much easier lives, be and do the same.

Prayer: "Lord, help me to remember Rick whenever things don't go the way I would like. Help me to reject the temptation to feel sorry for myself, to be angry, and instead help me to take up your grace, to praise you, remembering that you will use my disappointment and discomfort for good, and to give you glory in the moment and throughout the day. Amen."

Sally and Bill Romanoff
--by Sheila

I remember Sally Romanoff when I was a child as
always being friendly and outgoing. I didn't know that she also
wore many hats. Besides being a wife and mother, Sally was a
grocery storeowner, a representative to Connecticut
legislature, a floral designer and an orchid grower.

In 1918, when Sally was two weeks old, the Havunens,
moved to Canterbury from Brooklyn. Below is a picture of the

family, Sally is the little girl in the front row.

Eventually they settled in the center of town, the part
called "the Canterbury Green." At that time, the road from
Brooklyn was just a cart path and everyone in that area of
Canterbury placed their mailbox at the Green because the
mailman didn't go south past the Congregational Church.

She remembers that the Fourth of July was always a
big event in Canterbury and most of the townspeople met at
the Canterbury Green to celebrate.

There were lots of firecrackers and once a skyrocket
landed in her father's barn setting the haystacks on fire. Since
practically everyone in Town was at the celebration, there was

plenty of help to put out the fire and then everyone just went on with the activities.

As a girl, Sally, Marguerite Simpson and Margaret Robinson were pals and all went to 4H camp together. Malcolm Wibberley drove them there, along with many of the neighborhood children. Malcolm would also pick and deliver apples from his farm to all the schools in town.

Sally met her husband, Bill Romanoff, because he worked at the Frink and Wright store across the street from her house.

In 1935 Bill and Sally were married and in 1939 they bought the Frink and Wright store and became entrepreneurs. In the picture

to the right, Bill stands in front of the store with his son, Bob. In 1953, they sold it to Michael Pappas and went into the orchid business full time. Eventually, Michael bought Sally's family home (the Havunen property) and built what is now Better Val U.

Bill was on the building committee for the Dr. Helen

Baldwin School along with Arnold Kerr, Rev. William Tyler, Elva Lovell (everyone who went to school in the 50's and 60's remembers Mrs. Lovell) and Ralph Lovell. The school was built in 1947 with funds from the state, help from local citizens and donated materials.

Bill had a dream to grow orchids and started with one exotic plant. He worked days at the grocery store, but at night he would read everything he could to discover how to grow and hybridize orchids.

Orchid growers would not tell outsiders their growing secrets, so Bill and Sally had to figure out by trial and error how to grow them. In our day and age, orchids can quickly be cloned, but when the Romanoffs began, they had to learn how to grow individual plants.

They couldn't buy seeds, so they had to use orchid pollen. At first the pollen would get moldy and die, and finally they realized the growing medium had to be bacteria free-- even breathing on the soil would cause mold to form. They had to create a bacteria free area and use a sterilized case and tongs to work with the pollen.

Once the pollen sprouted and seedlings grew to the proper size, they separated them and put them in a container of California Redwood bark. Eventually, they began to take orders for their orchids and delivered them all over New

England.

They started with a small green house about 7x9 attached to the house, and over their fifty-year career in the orchid business, they built 11 full size greenhouses (some are the white buildings seen in picture to the left) and growers would come from all over the country to see their orchid farm.

There are more than 25,000 different varieties of orchids and it can take up to seven years to grow one orchid. They can live for many years and are often left to a relative in a will.

To enhance their business, Sally went to floral design school. In the 1960's Sally was elected as a Connecticut legislative representative for six years. She tells how she would deliver orchids to West Springfield, MA and then drive to

Hartford for the 10:00am legislative session.

In the small town of Canterbury, Sally shared, with her husband, the American dream. It started with the vision of one person and became a reality with a family's hard work.

In the picture below, taken four days before Sally died, from left to right, Sally, daughter Patty, son-in-law Jack and son Bobby

Below Sally as a teen in Canterbury

Smith Family
--by Steve

The Smiths had seven children. The ones I know of, Donald, Bill, Sid and Priscilla, were each a remarkable person, living productive and long lives.

Bill (P.B.) was the town's plumber—and an excellent one, always ready to help whenever he was called. He was active in politics and social life. He purchased the old train depot building, which had been moved to the junction of Butts Bridge Road and 169, and he converted it into his home. He was also a bear hunter in his younger days.

Priscilla was the first person in Canterbury to volunteer for the military when World War II started, joining the WACS. She held several political positions in Canterbury including Judge of Probate. And she was a talented author, as seen in the article above about Miss Lucy.

Sid (picture on right) was an adventurer, headstrong and body strong, unafraid of danger and challenge.

Donald was the pioneer, going to Northern Ontario in 1923 as a twenty-one year old young man to set up a trapline to support himself and his siblings. Sid, Bill and Priscilla all joined him there for various parts of the ten years he ran that trap line full time.

Donald wrote a book about their experiences, *The Great Trapline,* which is well worth reading; I recommend that you buy one from www.abebooks.com, or borrow a copy from the Canterbury library.

Since Donald is such a good writer, I will simply quote some passages from his book (with permission from the publisher, Les Editions Cantinales) to give you a taste of the Smith Siblings and their adventures.[5]

Beginnings

When Sid and I first explored the country to the east trying to blaze out a trap line, we ran into so much swamp that we made very little progress the first day. The second day we had to go through a cedar swamp and on the other side we came to a stream that was wide and deep. There was no timber on our side to make a bridge,

It was cold, below freezing, and there was a little snow on the ground. In spite of this, Sid took off all his cloths, threw his axe across the creek, plunged in and swam over.

On the other side there was a big spruce tree that leaned right across the creek. Standing there, bare-naked in the cold and wet, Sid chopped that tree down. He came running back across on the tree trunk, jumping over the limbs.

 I told him that with his rosy red skin and his hair and whiskers, he reminded me of a giant red squirrel. He was too cold to be in any mood for humor, but he was proud of his bridge. In the picture left, Sid is relaxing in front of one of the trap line cabins.

Incredible Provision and Protection

One of the most dangerous experiences I had in the bush was on a trip when the temperature to about 55 degrees

5 All the following material is used with verbal permission from publisher of *The Great Trapline*, Donald B. Smith, 2003, Les Editions Cantinales, Herst, Onterio, Canada

below zero. About four miles out of camp I had to cross a creek and, because it was so cold, I took no precautions.

I had not yet learned that in extreme cold the water level in a creek will fall, leaving an air space between the ice and the water. The present freeze had cracked and weakened the ice so that when I stepped on it, it gave way. In an instant, without any warning I found myself up to my arm pits in icy water.

I was carrying a rifle because I was badly in need of moose meat. In the excitement of the sudden breakthrough, I dropped the rifle but came to my senses and grabbed it just before it sank out of sight in the water.

My snow shoes were tied to my feet and I had a packsack on my back. I threw the rifle to shore, got my packsack off quickly, and threw it to shore. Then I struggled to lift my snow shoes, which had sunk into the mud. It took several minutes of frantic maneuvering to get my snow shoes out of the mud and to drag myself, chilled to the bone, out of that mess of broken ice, snow, mud and water.

This creek ran through a little moose meadow and the nearest trees were about 200 feet away. By the time I had collected my packsack, snow shoes, and gun, and ploughed thru the deep snow to the nearest tree, my clothes had frozen solid so that I could not bend my knees and elbows. My pants and coat were like a suit of icy armor and I was freezing fast.

I had to have a fire and quickly, but getting one started under these conditions was almost impossible. I always carried dry matches in a small bottle. My fingers were numb, but I managed to pull the cork from the bottle with my teeth.

Then I found that my fingers were too numb to scratch the match to light it. Finally, after holding the match with both hands and rubbing it back and forth across my axe I got it to light. Using the birch bark from my frozen packsack, I managed to get a good flame going.

However, the location of the fire was a poor one. I never should have started a fire under this big spruce tree, which had such low hanging limbs. The heat from the fire caused a big blob of snow to fall from one of the snow laden braches. It plopped onto the fire and completely extinguished it.

I was desperate. I knew that I had to have another fire, but had already used the little hand full of birch bark I always carried for emergency kindling.

I was by now so numb and cold that I was not thinking clearly. For some crazy reason, I began to think of my home in Connecticut. Then I remembered that when I left to come north, my sister Priscilla had given me a small can of sterno heat. I had not wanted to take it, but she had insisted; so, more or less out of regard for her, I had carried the little sterno can buried somewhere in my packsack for a couple of months.

I began to search or it, and much to my surprise I found it. There was no way I could open the lid, so I chopped thru it with my axe. I then moved out from under the tree, tramped down a place in the snow, laid down some spruce boughs on which I placed my can of sterno.

By now I was freezing to death. In slow, ponderous motions and with great effort I gathered some dead boughs from the big spruce. After breaking several matches in an effort to light one, I held three of them together. I rubbed them across the axe several times, and finally they burst into flames. I placed them on the sterno can and soon had a little fire going.

Stiff-legged and stiff-armed, I managed to break and cut more branches and sticks, which I piled on top. I kept at it

until I could no more. By now there was quite a good bile of firewood stacked over a spluttering flame. I broke some green spruce boughs and laid them in the snow and dropped down on them very close to the fire.

[editor's comment: note the three miraculous happenings here. At the needed moment, Bill remembered his sister, Priscilla (pictured on left with

Donald on his trap line) giving him the sterno; second he had it in his sack; third he was able to start a fire with it when there was no other possibility of doing so. This was protection from above, preserving his life when he should have died.]

Next thing I knew, I smelled burning wool. My fire was blazing nicely, and I was so close to it that one sleeve of my coat was starting to scorch. The heat had revived me somewhat.

I managed to get up and stand over the fire until my clothes were thawed out. Then I had to undress completely, hang my clothes on stakes as close to the fire as possible without burning them, and stand there naked at 55 degrees below zero. I turned round and round, roasting first one side and then the other, until I was warm enough to gather up some snow in my tea pail. When the snow was melted, I made tea; and nothing ever tasted so good as that hot tea.

Besides my clothes, I also had to dry out my packsack, moccasins, snow shoes and rifle. I think I was there about two hours. When I left, I swore that I would stop for nothing until I got into camp. But it was not to be so.

For days, I had carried my rifle trying to get a shot at a moose. Now, about two miles from the camp fire, I was hurrying along trying to get to the next camp. My head was down, and I was still cold. I heard a noise off to one side of the trail. Sure enough, about 100 yards away standing broad side to me, was a young cow moose. She had just risen from her bed in the snow. I had to have meat, so I shot her.

I built another big fire. Never did a man do such a quick and crude job of dressing out a moose. I threw a chunk of the meat into my packsack and went wearily back to the trail. It was long after dark when I got back into camp.

Provision in the Teeth of a Storm

One day I was snow shoeing along my trapline, facing a terrible blizzard. The storm was howling out of the west and I was heading right into it. I would soon reach the end of this trapline. At that point I would turn around and retrace my steps seven miles back to my main camp. All I could think of was what a relief it would be to turn and have the storm at my back. Fighting the strong storm, with the snow swirling in my face, I did not hear or see anything else. However, all at once, I sensed the presence of something. I looked around.

My eyes were so filled with snow that I couldn't see clearly, but I didn't need much sight to spot the tremendous bull moose which rose up out of his bed just to the right of the trail. I whirled to meet him, throwing the mitt off my right hand, and jabbing my rifle almost into his shoulder, I pulled the trigger and killed him in one shot.

What a bad time I has skinning him and cutting out the meat in that raging storm! I knew it would do little good to try to build a fire with such a wind blowing. Therefore, I worked with all the speed that I could muster.

He seemed awfully tough when I was cutting him up. I have killed several larger ones but never did I find one which

 seemed so tough. There was no way you could eat it as a steak. I tried it in a stew but Sid said that even the stew was tough. We gave some to a French friend who said, "She good but she liddle bit a hard!"

On our next trip to town we bought a meat grinder. But even after putting the meat through the grinder it still was tough. In picture on left, Sid holds a pair of large moose antlers.

Saved by a Branch

Once in early November I came down to cross the river in the midst of a howling blizzard. There were four inches of snow on the ground and lots more falling. My canoe was stored bottom upward. I pulled it out from underneath the snow, turned it right side up, threw my packsack and axe in, and keeping the paddle in my hand to use as a cane to keep from slipping down the bank, I lifted the bow of the canoe up onto a fallen tree.

The snow and ice on the log made it easy to start it sliding towards the river. I jumped hurriedly over the log to follow the canoe, but in doing so I lost my hold on it and fell flat on my face. The canoe picked up speed and sped towards the river. Before I could regain my feet, it reached the water. Its momentum and the wind carried it half way across.

As I watched in dismay, the wind and the current turned the canoe, and it headed down the center of the river.

I could not afford to lose my axe or my packsack with my tea pale, traps and first aid kit. Also, I could not afford to lose the canoe, which was my only means of crossing the river between camps.

The current was extremely swift here, but I knew that about a quarter of a mile downstream the river broadened and the current there was not so strong. I threw down the paddle and ran along the riverbank, hoping to get ahead of the canoe and eventually to swim out to it. There was some ice and slush in the river that was slowing down the canoe to some extend.

I started to undress as I ran. The blizzard was cold and wild but I gave it no thought. I threw off my mittens, hat, coat, shirt, and then my undershirt. I could not stop running to remove my boots and pants. I was having all that I could do to keep up with the canoe.

When I thought I could run not further, by some good fortune a freakish gust of wind hit the canoe and turned it towards shore. It was coming right in, straight at me. I held on to a tree on the bank and reached out to catch it.

Just then another freakish gust hit it and turned it away from my hands and back out into the river. I continued my race along the shore. The canoe had now reached the quiet water but was being driven by the wind towards a strong current which led into a series of rapids. I knew that if it reached those rapids it was lost.

Again, a gust of wind hit it and turned it towards my shore. I ran for the water. As I ran, I pulled over a dead young spruce tree and yanked it up by its roots. I stepped down into the water with the tree in my hand. The canoe came almost within my grasp, when the wind hit it again and started taking it away. This time, however, I reached out with the spruce sapling. It was just long enough for one of the roots to catch in the stern, and I was able to pull it to shore.

I was by now mighty cold and almost exhausted. I got my axe out of the canoe, cut down a dead spruce, and hewed out a crude paddle. Half-naked and in the storm, I paddled back upstream to our crossing place and tied the canoe to a tree.

Next, I retraced my steps down the riverbank, retrieving the clothing I had thrown off in my wild run. After dressing myself, I slid the canoe very carefully into the river and crossed over.

In the picture on the left, Donald carries a caribou he shot on one of his trips around the trap line. You can see how strong he is, as he carries it with such ease.

Bill's Bear

My brother Bill, pictured below, wanted to get a bear.

One fall he was following a trail through a thick stand of balsam and spruce trees. He happened to look up, and there, coming around a bend towards him was a huge black bear. The bear saw him and stopped in surprise. Bill didn't know what the bear was going to do, and he didn't wait to find out. He whipped out his 38-caliber pistol and with one quick shot he dropped the bear.

The bear was wounded but far from dead. Before Bill could get in another shot, it leaped up and dove under a great mass of windfalls — a jumble of trees blown over and twisted together by a violent storm. Bill hated to leave a wounded animal and he also wanted that bear, so he very carefully worked his way up unto the pile of trees, peering through the branches trying to locate his bear.

All at once a rotten limb broke under his feet and he went crashing through. As he neared the ground, broken limbs gouged and scratched his legs. He thought the bear was attacking him.

As his toes touched the ground, he sprang up with such force that it carried him back up and through the hole he had made and rolled him off unto the ground. He had had enough and got out of there in a hurry.

Two weeks later, coming over that same trail, he smelled the terrible odor of rotting flesh, so he knew that the bear had died. He did not bother to look for it as he guessed that neither the hide nor the meat would be of any value.

It Was Not All Adventure

Many nights we sat in camp by candle light darning socks, sewing on buttons, and mending our clothes, moccasins and snow shoes also had to be repaired, knives and axes sharpened, and guns cleaned and oiled. So many things had to be done in addition to the routine of chopping of wood, cooking, skinning animals and stretching furs and washing dishes and making the bed.

The first year I was alone, it was hard to get used to the fact that there was no one else to do any of these things. Everything that needed to be done I must do by myself.

Then there were the long days on the trapline when there was no excitement. There were days of breaking out the snow shoe trail--all 80 miles of it--after a heavy storm, when it seemed as though there wasn't enough strength left to get to the next camp. Even with snow shoes, each step sinks into the snow, 8 inches or more.

When two men are traveling together, they take turns breaking the trail. A man alone must do it all by himself. I guess it was the hardest job a trapper had to do. Breaking trail from one camp to the next meant leaving one camp before daylight, and getting to the next one after dark

The Profits

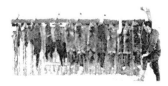In the winter of 1925-26, Sid and I caught 27 beaver, 56 mink, 16 martins, 94 ermine, 3 otter and 2 lynxes. The fur sold for $1,972--in those days this was quite a fortune when the going wage for a laborer was about 80 dollars a month. In the picture on the left, Donald stands next some of his furs. For 10 years, the income from this trap line played a role in not only supporting me, but my mother, 3 brothers and 4 sisters.

Tony Marquis
--by Sheila

Former Canterbury resident, Tony Marquis, told me that what we know as Goodwin Road today was originally Old Windham Lane on the Canterbury side of Little River.

In 1944 Arthur and Irene Marquis and their eleven children (Robert, Arthur, Jr., Tony, Lawrence, Henry, Ellen, May, Ruth, Julia, Ada and Dora) moved to Canterbury into a home that was built in the late 1700's. Although the original barn is gone, the house is still standing today.

Irene's mother found the house for the family; it was a big house, but it had no heat, no water, no phone and no electricity. Electricity was available, but residents had to pay for a pole to be put up on the road, and the Marquis could not afford that until after World War II.

As for water, it was the biggest child's job to bring the water up the hill from the spring to the house. Arthur was a good mason and built all the stonewalls on the property. Their only neighbors were the Miller family.

The children loved to swim and fish in the river, seen here on left, where they would catch bullheads and trout 10-12 inches long, put them into a wash tub, bring them home and release them in their spring fed pond to re-catch them when they needed to eat.

As you can imagine, with all those children to feed, they had a big garden by the house. There were apple trees in the lower lot and the apples were picked and put in barrels in the cellar for eating all winter. Irene made jelly and jams and canned the vegetables from their garden.

In the winter they would ice skate along the frozen edge of Little River and make toboggans using big sheets of

288

tin that Arthur brought home from Brand-Rex that were thrown away. They would bend the edges down along the sides and back and nail two boards to the front, add a piece of rope and down the hill they went.

The children went to the Westminster one-room school house and Tony remembers Mrs. Triplehorn, Mrs. Colburn and Mrs. Bingham as his teachers. A few of his school mates were Russell Fault, Ali Galasyn, Joyce Eastlund and the Romanoff children.

When Tony was young, Bob Miller would drive the children to school in his car until busses were used to pick them up. He remembers Halloween parties at the old Meeting Hall that used to be next to Calvary Chapel where they played Halloween games and had peanut hunts.

Below the Marquis property was a log chute. The children would gather along the river's edge in the spring to watch the logs slide down the chute, splash into the river and then float downstream to be used by a saw mill to make wooden coffins.

As you can imagine, the children had to sleep with their siblings, but Tony wanted his own bed. Grandma Bennett gave the Marquis family a feather mattress when Tony was four or five. It was set on the floor in the upstairs hallway and he slept facing the two bedrooms at the end of the hall.

One night he woke up and saw three American Indian women dressed in long white dresses walking toward him down the hallway. They stopped and stood all in a row by the foot of his bed. He was scared and hid his head under the covers, but eventually he peeked out and they disappeared into the air.

He jumped out of bed ran into his mother's room to tell her about the ladies, but she thought Tony was seeing things. Throughout his childhood, he would often see them in the hall at night, but would just cover his head until the three lady ghosts disappeared and he would go back to sleep. As he grew older he would occasionally see the three ladies in the hallway, but after he came home from the Army, they never returned.

When Tony was a teenager, he and his brothers and his father were asked to clean out the Westminster church because the members were going to paint the inside and outside of the church. They came across old books, papers and an old family bible (which he returned to the family).

He was looking through the bible and an old postcard fell out. He picked it up, turned it over and was shocked to discover the photo was of the three American Indian ladies dressed in white that he saw in the hallway as a child. The photo showed the ladies standing on the front steps of his house.

He later learned the three ladies had lived in his house and had been good neighbors. They would make and sell baskets for a living. They cut reeds, dried them and wove them into baskets and would sell them to neighbors and even travel to other towns to sell them. A mystery somewhat solved.

In the Army he worked at Fort Dix assembling missiles and later was a squad leader in Hawaii after the Korean War. Everything he saw he wanted to know what it was and how it worked. He learned everything so he could be in charge, as in the Army "Being the boss is the only place to be".

After his time in the Army, he worked at Federal Paper Board, but one day he was driving by Martin's Garage in Willimantic and noticed it was closed. He heard the owners were looking for someone to re-open it so he interviewed with them. Although he had not worked as a mechanic for a job, he told them he had worked on a farm as a child and could repair the vehicles and equipment, so he was confident he could do the job.

Back on the farm, as the youngest boy, it had been his job to hand all the tools to his father and older brothers as they fixed the equipment, so he learned how to repair many types of vehicles. He was hired and ran the garage for ten years until the gas crisis came and the garage was closed down. He then worked at Brand-Rex. As usual, he learned how to operate all the machines on the floor which made him the "go-to" man.

His pursuit of excellence extended to his present home.

He bought one of the old mill houses in Willimantic and completely renovated it from top to bottom to suit his needs.

He loved growing up in Canterbury along the river. He and his brothers and sisters were down at the river all the time in the summer enjoying the warm weather, fishing and swimming. In the winter they were skating and sledding. Although it was a difficult for the family to manage with eleven children and Tony had lots of chores, he also had fun, enjoyed both nature and growing up in the country.

One final picture of a class at Gayhead School in the early 1900s, maybe a reunion, as some look rather old to be students. By guess I only recognize those seated in the middle row, as it is made up of my (Steve) ancestors, left to right, Maud, Malcolm, Florence and Walter Wibberley.

Made in the USA
Columbia, SC
13 July 2017